WHEN NOBODY'S HOME:

WHEN NOBODY'S HOME:

**Reveal and Heal the Missing Pieces of
Childhood Trauma and Painful Experiences**

Break the Cycle of Dependency

By

Michael S. Oden, M.A.,
Behavioral Specialist

authorHOUSE®

AuthorHouse™
1663 Liberty Drive
Bloomington, IN 47403
www.authorhouse.com
Phone: 1 (800) 839-8640

Editor: Deborah Drake/Authentic Writing Provokes www.authenticwritingprovokes.com
Copyeditor: Nora Tamada/Fresh Eye Editing www.fresheyeediting.com
Cover Design: Erica Stanton www.ericastanton.com

Published by AuthorHouse   01/22/2016

ISBN: 978-1-4969-1966-3 (sc)
ISBN: 978-1-4969-1965-6 (hc)
ISBN: 978-1-4969-1964-9 (e)

Library of Congress Control Number: 2014910749

Print information available on the last page.

A SPECIAL FOREWORD

Michael Oden is the sixth of eleven children, the seventh being a twin brother and I am proud to be his older sister who also doubled as mom from time to time. When I think back to those chaotic times of growing up in a very full house on 11 acres in Woodbury, Minnesota, it surprises me how clearly I recall each of my siblings. It was a very noisy household of nine boys, two girls and, over a period of 13 years, 173 group home children placed by the courts in our licensed group home Depending on their social disposition, some stayed for one day and others for ten years.

Michael stood out because he rarely spoke and when he did, as a younger child, he stuttered. My sense of him is that he was observing what was going on around him. He was easy-going and undemanding but never forgotten because his twin spoke for him. "He wants a P&B sandwich with grape jelly". "Is that what you want Mike?" A nod of the head indicated an affirmative answer. He seemed to often be outside of the fray, a good place to be in our house, but adept at getting along with the many personalities at any given time.

When I had my own children, I appreciated how distinct they were from each other as well. As they entered school, I realized the need to advocate for them and their peers, as well, in order for them to benefit from the resources available to those "in the know. My background as the oldest girl, a product of the 1960s, and my early work as a public health nurse in a stressed urban city somehow came together and I began working with parents and the public schools on issues of access and equity. Organizing, listening and endless hours of committee meetings led to three terms on an elected Board of Education. When a position in the State Assembly opened up in 2007, I was asked to serve.

It saddens me to say as a lawmaker that the progress over the last half century in the United States' drug war has been a complete failure. After spending over a trillion dollars on our efforts to eradicate drugs and substance abuse from our culture, we have few successes to show for our efforts. In reality, our focus on punitive measures over treatment has only made the problems worse. Families and communities are torn apart and non-violent substance abusers are sent to prison with violent criminals in most states. Upon exiting prison, the issues that lead to their initial drug use are still unresolved, and now these individuals must also overcome the stigma of being ex-convicts.

As a state legislator, my job is to use all of the information at my disposal to set policies that will do the greatest good for the greatest number of residents in the state I serve as an elected official. While strides have been made in many areas, we have tragically failed to address the substance abuse epidemic in our country. Legislators need to recognize the failure of our current policies, and completely change course on this issue. Politicians are only as good as the people who elect them, so we as a people need to demand change. The reasons we need a new approach to treating substance abuse and dependency are both humanitarian and economic. If we are to maximize our potential as a people, we need to ensure that all of our citizens are healthy and able to contribute to our society.

My own political career started years ago, not in the New Jersey State Assembly, but as a school board member. My goals have always been about helping the people in my care to improve their lives. I am not surprised that Michael shares this characteristic with me. Growing up as we did enhanced Michael's natural ability to connect with others and his genuine interest in others has been essential in the development of his Needs Based Method. While understanding the method is of chief importance, I think it also helps to understand the man behind it.

In his capacity as a counselor and a Deputy Probation Officer for the state of California since 1998, he has always gone above and beyond the standard requirements. In his eyes, every client was once a person with unlimited potential and possibilities, who missed receiving the best foundational building blocks needed to become a happy, healthy, emotionally stable person who gets to choose their own path in life.

What he strives to do is heal the impact of early childhood traumas that propelled a person to choose drugs and alcohol as the way to deal with their pain. Surely, seeing so many children from broken homes either respond to the nurturing offered or witnessing others run away from the safety, structure and stability offered made a lasting impression. It has impacted the way he is as a person, a partner, a father and a counselor and has dramatically affected his work as a Deputy Probation Officer. While he's not exactly taking in foster children as our parents did for 13 years, he is effectively providing that same quality of compassionate stability and support to the adults he serves. If more in the counseling and social work fields saw through his eyes, how would it affect the healing journey that their clients in recovery experience?

Michael Oden's Needs Based Method® is exactly the kind of innovation that we need to address Nationwide substance dependency. As any capable problem solver knows, the key to solving a problem is first identifying its cause. This practical line of reasoning serves as the basis for the Needs Based Method (R). Only through understanding what we each need to achieve emotional health, can one ever hope to be free. I recommend this book to anyone who has been affected either personally or indirectly by substance dependency. Michael Oden has spent nearly two decades in the trenches working with substance abusers and his method has proven successful time and time again. It's unlikely that we will ever see a perfect cure for substance abuse, but Michael's 80% success rate is the best that

I've ever come across. This book and the approach it offers is the kind of solution that our country needs.

If you find it helpful, I hope that you will spread the word and champion the Needs Based Method as a tool for long term recovery and long-lasting change. Put this book in the hands of people with influence, or who work with those in recovery, that more people might not only get clean and clear of their addictive behavior but also become emotionally free.

~ Mila M. Jasey, Member of the New Jersey General Assembly,
27th Legislative District

TABLE OF CONTENTS

INTRODUCTION

WHEN CHEMICAL DEPENDENCY BECOMES A SURVIVAL MECHANISM

What causes a person to choose drugs and alcohol as a coping mechanism for survival?

My goal in writing this book is to not only help the reader understand how and why individuals begin to depend on drug use, but to truly understand how the early socialization of family dynamics plays a major role in the decisions an individual will make throughout life.

After fifteen years, 8,000+ interviews, and more than 30,000+ hours of working with my clients, I have my best answer and a suggested strategy for working to help heal those in recovery from addictive behaviors and substance abuse.

From the time we begin cognitive thinking we begin learning how to socialize and survive. Ideally, every child born would have nurturing caregivers who primed them for a successful life, but the reality is more often something different. Ideally, home is experienced as a safe place to be for comfort and connection, but what if home is a place of chaos and instability, uncertainty and abuse? What might a person do to cope and survive in that kind of environment?

We, as individuals, are deeply impacted by the felt (social/emotional) experience we have of family in childhood. A person who grows up in a family that is basically emotionally and physically safe has a higher probability of living in the world with confidence and a strong emotional foundation. This individual is more likely to have supportive peers, establish healthy intimate relationships, and nurture and raise a family of their own because this future adult does not need to second guess their actions. They will mirror their own experiences.

My experience, in regards to this book, has been more about traditional family dynamics that are patriarchal in nature. It is important for me to mention the reality of how the landscape of the nuclear family has changed over the years. Whatever the family dynamic, the bottom line is for the caretaker to meet the majority of the child's needs. *By showing up (being present), the caretaker's impact on the child's self-worth, purpose, and meaning about self is priceless.*

On the other hand, if an individual comes from a family dynamic where many social/emotional needs are not met and there are various forms of abuse in the home, then this individual will have a greater likelihood of living in the world feeling uncertain about who they are or how to relate to others on a healthy social/emotional level. They may view the world as an unpredictable and unsafe place. They will not know how to meet their own social/emotional needs much less those of their children, because this person has never experienced that kind of (life-affirming) behavior. They are prone to making decisions that involve harming others, using illicit drugs, engaging in criminal behavior, and having emotional detachment from their own family members, friends, or children.

The "behind the scenes" behavior in early family dynamics is where long-term damage is done to a young psyche. Therefore, it is always my intention when in a counseling role to understand where the trauma first occurred for my clients, for often that is where emotional development gets stunted or continues through a warped "filter" of their personal experiences.

As a Deputy Probation Officer, I chose to be candid with my clients from the start. With neutrality and diplomacy, I asked more personal questions of my clients than some of my peers. And what effect did that approach yield? This direct, yet benevolent, approach gained me their trust quickly and they often told stories about the pain of their childhood in the first session. I heard about how it made them feel and behave and develop as an adult.

So as the years passed and the more stories I heard, the more I began to see how a missing father impacted these men (man-child) and women (woman-child) on my case load. I began to piece together how not having a father, and having only a mother who then needed to work, allowed for the child to wander aimlessly in a world with few to no boundaries.

This early "freedom" was part of a setup for future crisis. This kind of early freedom allowed that child to more easily say yes to try drugs, join a gang, participate in delinquent behavior, believe he could do whatever he wanted, and continue criminal behavior as an adult. These behaviors and the consequences of them were never questioned until it was brought to their attention some ten to forty years later by the dialogues they would have with me as their assigned Deputy Probation Officer.

Did this have to be their lot in life? I say no. And in publishing this book I seek to cause a beneficial ripple in the professional fields that I care deeply about. I do my work as a Deputy Probation Officer and a Counselor with as much energy and commitment today as I always have.

My years of service during the years that California funded Proposition 36 were a pivotal time and many good things came out of taking on that tough yet demanding assignment.

What is California Proposition 36?

Prior to 2001, my work as a Deputy Probation Officer involved working with a variety of clients that included drug and alcohol offenders, but in September of 2002 I was transferred to a caseload that was specifically focused on alcohol and drug offenders. These individuals were eligible for a rehabilitation program funded by the State of California called Proposition 36, the Substance Abuse and Crime Prevention Act of 2000. More commonly referred to as "Prop 36," this was an initiative statute that permanently changed the state law to allow qualifying defendants convicted of nonviolent drug offenses to receive a grant of probation and enroll in a drug treatment program instead of going to county jail or state prison.

Failure to complete the treatment program, or violation of any other term or condition of their probation, meant that their grant of probation could be revoked. In the event that happened, the defendant might be required to serve an additional sentence, which could include county jail or prison time. Prop 36 was funded between 2001 and 2008. I worked with Prop 36 clients for nearly seven years.

This shift in my caseload could have ended my career as a Deputy Probation Officer, but it turned out to be a blessing in disguise. Where most of my peers might quickly burn out and seek to be transferred, I found that I was suited to work with this particular type of client. When I was transferred to the Proposition 36 caseload, approximately 300+ files had been dormant for over a year. My initial responsibility would be to find these people, orientate them regarding their probation conditions, and begin the supervision process.

As I looked at the stacks of files I had inherited, I decided that I would use this as an opportunity to try the unconventional behavioral techniques I was learning at that time. And because so many of my new clients responded, I knew I was onto something important. As the years passed and the interviews mounted, I learned how the lack of social/emotional needs being met affected human behavior. Being a Deputy Probation Officer is hardly glamorous work; nonetheless, I thoroughly enjoyed what I was engaged in and I was effective. I can honestly say that the next seven years were an exciting time for me. The work I did amounted to tens of thousands of hours of experience and provided me with the opportunity to apply my preferred techniques and really come to understand why my approach worked as well as it did.

As a Deputy Probation Officer, I worked wholeheartedly to assure my clients' chances of completing their grants of probation, staying out of the penal system for good, and reconnecting with their families in an empowered way was increased. I worked with clients who were eighteen to seventy-five years of age. These are what society refers to as "Adult Children" or "grown-ass men." My role was to monitor my clients for eighteen months to assure that they did not violate the requirements of their probation or break other laws that might land them in prison. I could have stopped my line of questioning once I obtained the necessary personal, professional, and criminal information. Yet, I always went above and beyond with clients who were willing to engage in a more in-depth conversation with me regarding their drug offense(s). The behavioral techniques I used worked quickly, consistently, and revealed a direct relationship between their criminal offenses and childhood neglect.

To date, I have conducted over 8,000+ interviews with alcohol and drug offenders, regarding their drug/alcohol dependency. All had several basic characteristics in common that propelled these individuals to start using drugs at a very young age in most instances, which would continue for many years into adulthood. With that in mind, this book reviews and explains the "Needs Based Method®" of alcohol and drug abuse and how this approach brings to question the reason "why."

When I interviewed these individuals, I discovered that they were what I would refer to as a "man-child," or "woman-child." I refer to them as adult-children because of early traumatic events that dramatically stifled their social/emotional growth. Their behavior became more about survival than living to their full potential as human beings. Because of their early life-diminishing experiences, their childlike behavior would continue to manifest itself in their adult world.

I understood that these individuals were arrested for drug and alcohol offenses; however, I also believed there had to be more to their using illicit drugs than what was being presented to me. I was not well-versed in Twelve-Step Programs and Support Groups like Alcoholics Anonymous (AA), Cocaine Anonymous (CA), or Narcotics Anonymous (NA). Early in my years as a Deputy Probation Officer, prior to my formal education and training as a counselor, I knew I needed more understanding about this word "addiction." So I decided to investigate deeper, to get to the truth behind a client's drug use. From the beginning I wanted to make my work more interesting and satisfying personally, but mainly I wanted my clients to complete their probation and be "out of the system" for good!

It became clear that class and money did not protect a person from getting hooked on illicit drugs, and it is still the case that it does not matter how much education a person has or how financially secure they are. Having access to more resources helps, but this is not the common theme or the "through-line" where drug/alcohol dependency occurs in the stories I hear. The most common denominator—rich or poor, educated or not—is the emotional, physical, or social absence of or "neglect" by a caretaker, or *When Nobody's Home.*

There are those who don't use drugs until later in response to a tragic life event such as a divorce, loss of a job, death of a loved one, but for every person who is dependent on drugs/alcohol as a coping mechanism, there is something that triggers an overwhelming sensation of helplessness.

What causes a person to use drugs if it "really" is not beneficial for them?

I was determined to go behind the scenes with my clients and come to understand what specific social/emotional need(s) were being met by consuming drugs day after day and year after year. Otherwise, why would a person choose this type of behavior? I had a difficult time believing that these individuals had some disease of the mind, that they would never recover fully, and that to avoid relapse they would need to attend support meetings—literally for the rest of their lives. A lifetime of meetings couldn't be the only workable solution, could it?

The first question I ask every client is, "What was your drug of choice?" After their initial response, I pose my next question, "Why do you think you started to use drugs?" Common responses include "because I wanted to," "because I felt like it," "because if feels good." But the response most interesting of all to me and also the most popular is: "I don't know, no one has ever asked me that question before."

As the interviews continued, I eventually got to the "core" reason why an individual would begin to use narcotics for any length of time. I discovered that the majority of my clients began to use drugs between ten to thirteen years of age. I would ask, "What was going on in the home at that time for you to begin using drugs?" The most popular response I received time and time again was that there was no one home. What does that mean? It meant that there was literally or figuratively no parental figure in the home to provide positive mentoring and support.

This "nobody home" condition can come in a variety of ways, such as divorce, the death of the father, imprisonment, or being socially/ emotionally absent within the home. Therefore, the social/emotional responsibility usually fell on the mother, who was typically working extra jobs and didn't have time to meet the social/emotional needs of the client as a child. In some cases the children were being raised by other relatives or in foster care.

I grew up in a large family that was also a group home for a thirteen-year period to 173 kids, mostly inner-city boys aged eight to seventeen; with so many pseudo-sibling and being raised with a brother who had Down's Syndrome, I learned how to be especially compassionate with those who were different and those whose initial home life had been less than ideal, troubled, and colored by abuse and/or neglect. What does someone in this scenario instinctively do? He looks elsewhere to get those social/ emotional needs met.

Drug use typically begins for one or more reasons: to either numb emotional pain, enhance a behavior that has been denied, or gain acceptance from other individuals who offer a sense of belonging (dysfunctional as it may be). Understand this reality: When a child is ignored or abused early in life by primary caregivers, the possibility that he will take on a belief system that he is unworthy is highly likely. He will take this belief system into adulthood, and it is this belief system that destroys potential relationships, child-rearing capabilities, and basic life-affirming social interaction with others in the adult world.

Where does the Needs Based Method® come from?

I was given the opportunity to work with drug and alcohol offenders and then Proposition 36 clients, specifically, for over eight years as a Deputy Probation Officer in the State of California. I wanted to know the truth behind their drug dependency. To me, it involved more than just labeling someone an addict for the rest of their life. This way of looking at the drug problem did not sit well with me. So, I decided to apply different behavioral approaches that I had learned to see if I could facilitate real healing and solid change in a person branded a "drug addict" by the criminal justice system for their victimless crime. I find the concept of "victimless crime" to be a bit of an oxymoron as I work directly with people whom I think of as being the victims.

Early in my career as a Deputy Probation Officer, even before I returned to school to formally educate myself as a Counselor, I found my key therapeutic tools in the writings and modalities developed by Joseph Campbell, Carolyn Myss, and Marshall Rosenberg.

The Needs Based Method® that I developed is one of my primary tools in working with clients. The method continues to evolve, but it remains a foundational philosophy for me in relating to people whether I am in the role of Deputy Probation Officer, counselor, peer, parent, or simply a fellow human being. It was born out of my appreciation for the work of Joseph Campbell on The Hero's Journey, Carolyn Myss on Sacred Contracts and Archetypes, and my deep study of Marshall Rosenberg's Non-Violent Communication Model.

What is "The Hero's Journey" and why must it be taken?

I appreciate the writings of Joseph Campbell and his discovery of the central theme he developed called the "monomyth" or "The Hero's Journey." This fundamental pattern is found in many narratives from around the world in which storytelling is used to learn the meaning of one's life. During our lifetime, one way or another, we are destined to take our own personal journey that will either make us stronger or will break us.

Therefore, it is the individual's responsibility to understand the meaning of that journey by the experiences involved. It is here that I discovered the reappearance of certain themes time and time again with the interviews I conducted. For example, the underlying theme that surrounded the clients I interviewed was that a greater part of these individuals were fatherless and I discovered how growing up without a father impacted the behavior of these clients.

Every person born is presented the chance to take their Hero's Journey willingly or when they find themselves in a situation that requires their attention. If a person says yes to the journey, then they will encounter people or situations that will guide them on this adventure. They will also make the decision to go forward with an important task and learn who will assist them and who will not. The "Hero" will learn about their strengths and weaknesses. Once the necessary knowledge and skills are gained, the "Hero" is ready to face their ultimate fear, also known as "The Supreme Ordeal." Once accomplished, they gain the reward and return back to a familiar world. However, the "Hero" is a different person because of what was learned, and can now share their experiences to help others.

If the Hero's Journey is not taken then there will not be any personal, spiritual, or emotional growth for that person. The life that you lead will forever be stunted because of your inability to step out of your comfort zone or challenge yourself. You will be forever frozen or trapped in your given situation, fearful of taking your own Hero's journey.

As the final chapter illustrates more in-depth, The Hero's Journey can be applied to a client wanting to break free of drug dependency for good. The way I described The Hero's Journey as it related to my client's personal histories always caused "aha" moments that accelerated their understanding of how their drug use started, the impact drug use had on their family members and their relationships, and what they needed to do to become truly clean and emotionally free.

What are Archetypes and why are they important?

I also appreciated the writings of Caroline Myss, whose bestselling book *Sacred Contracts: Awakening Your Divine Potential* poses the ideas: "We all want to know: Why are we here?" "What is our mission in life?" and "Why do some people find their mission easily while others struggle for a clue?"(Myss, p.1) What I found impactful was how she used "archetypes" to identify certain behavioral patterns, beliefs, and relationships. An archetype is a set of unconscious behavior patterns that are derived from historical roles in life such as "Mother," "Rescuer," "Knight," and "Teacher." Archetypes are universally understood symbols or patterns of behavior.

Reading Carolyn Myss, I came to understand that knowing your primary archetype helps you to understand why certain relationships, beliefs, and values have been necessary in your life and why you have taken on certain specific behaviors that either enhanced your life or diminished your life. For example, over the years of interviewing drug/alcohol dependent individuals, I witnessed consistent behavioral patterns that my clients displayed which were congruent with the archetypes of the "Orphan Child," "Wounded Child," "Rebel," "Saboteur," "Victim," "Prostitute," and "Slave." Their perception of themselves was indicative of their behavioral archetype.

Using myself as an example, the primary archetype displayed when I am with a client is that of the "Healer." "The Healer archetype manifests as a passion to serve others in the form of repairing the body, mind, and spirit. . . . Essential characteristics include an inherent strength and the ability to assist people in transforming their pain into a healing process, as well as having the 'wiring' required to channel the energy needed to generate physical or emotional changes."(Myss, p.390)

Every archetype has a light and dark side/expression and archetypes are in essence neutral. Our early life experiences affect how we behave and the choices we make for our benefit or to our detriment. Knowing and understanding your archetype allows you to see what part of your behavior plays that role and what you can do to change it.

Non-Violent Communication: Why does it work so well?

Another effective tool that I rely upon is Marshall Rosenberg's Theory of Non-Violent Communication. Using this technique with my clients over the years, I discovered how effective this tool was at getting to the core of the social/emotional needs that were not being met during their early stages of development. As the years passed, I developed my own style and rhythm of Non-Violent Communication which has morphed into what I now call "The Needs Based Method."

Over the years, I became more skilled in using these methodologies for "emotional/social awareness" and "conflict resolution," and I decided to enroll into graduate school in August 2010 to obtain a Master's Degree in Counseling Psychology. The collective experiences of my own childhood, having a special needs brother, and growing up as a pseudo-sibling to 173 foster children over a thirteen-year period, helped make me a more compassionate Deputy Probation Officer.

I have heard almost every tragic story imaginable from my clients. Because of my nature, I wanted to see if I could successfully get them to take their past events (painful experiences) and destructive behavior and put it behind them for good. I was certain that if they could do that they wouldn't need to continue consuming illicit drugs and alcohol to hide from their feelings. I wanted them to experience living without blame, shame, or guilt.

Once the "truth" was uncovered and the healing began they experienced a value shift in their lives and they could be transformed by the information that was offered to them in a non-judgmental way. They could stop feeling broken (shame/guilt) and believing they were unworthy. I am a firm believer that we are put on this planet for a reason. My belief is, while I am here I have the fortunate opportunity to contribute to as many lives as I can with the tools I have been given. There is nothing more gratifying and pleasing to me than when a client returns after the initial session and informs me that they have a new awareness and understanding about their personal journey and a new pattern of behavior that is more life-serving.

Non-Violent Communication (NVC) is a model for peaceful or diplomatic communication that often functions as a conflict resolution method. It focuses on three characteristics of communication: The first is referred to as self-empathy (defined as a profound and empathetic awareness of one's own inner understanding of self). The second is called empathy (defined as listening to another with deep compassion). And the third is truthful self-expression (defined as expressing oneself authentically in a way that is likely to inspire compassion in others). NVC was developed in the 1960s by Clinical Psychologist Dr. Marshall Rosenberg, PhD and is also referred to as Compassionate Communication or Collaborative Communication.

NVC is rooted in the idea that all human beings have the capacity for compassion and only resort to violence or behavior that harms others when they don't recognize more effective strategies for meeting needs. Habits of thinking and speaking that lead to the use of violence (psychological and physical) are learned through culture. NVC theory supposes all human behavior stems from attempts to meet universal human needs and that these needs are never in conflict. Rather, conflict arises when strategies for meeting needs clash. NVC proposes that if people can identify their needs, the needs of others, and the feelings that surround these needs, harmony can be achieved.

While NVC is supposedly taught as a process of communication designed to improve compassionate connection to others, it has also been interpreted as a spiritual practice, a set of values, a parenting technique, an educational method, and a worldview.

My experience of using NVC principles and techniques with clients—who were essentially strangers to me at first meetings—was so immediately effective that I adopted this approach very early in my career. I have been using it ever since and developed my own personal protocol and process based on NVC methodology known as the Needs Based Method®

The Needs Inventory Checklist: What person doesn't want their needs met?

In my experience working with drug and alcohol offenders, I discovered that the sooner I was able to have a client complete a self-assessment tool that I call the "Needs Inventory" sheet, the better subsequent sessions went. Ideally, this self-assessment process occurred in the first session. The Needs Inventory had a profound effect on clients because the sheet itself allowed clients to actually see a list of needs that were not met at any given period in their life and what individual was unable to meet those needs.

The "Needs Inventory" is a checklist of needs that human beings require on a basic social and emotional level. When the majority of an individual's needs are met by the primary caretakers and the environment in which a person lives, that person will tend to view their life as one of security and predictability. However, if the majority of those needs are not met then the individual will view the world as an unsafe, unreliable, and inconsistent experience. It is because of the lack of these needs that the individual will be unable to obtain any self-worth, self-respect, purpose, integrity, values, and meaning in regards to how the individual navigates his life.

When a need has not been met in the past it becomes a point of pathology (suffering) for the client. For example, in the chart that follows, the graph informs you what basic social/emotional needs are required for an individual to mature into an emotionally healthy and productive adult. What I discovered as a Deputy Probation Officer was that the majority of the clients that I interviewed did not have most of these needs met during their formative years.

By the time an individual becomes my client, he has experienced a lifetime of emotional suffering that is directly attributed to his years of drug abuse/dependency. These individuals have been dependent on alcohol and drugs in some cases since the age of ten. In addition, these individuals have learned how to survive in a world that has shown them that their life is not emotionally or physically safe, neither stable nor predictable. Therefore, they learned how to survive and react to their world, wondering when the next traumatic event would occur. <u>I wanted them to see that change could be for good.</u>

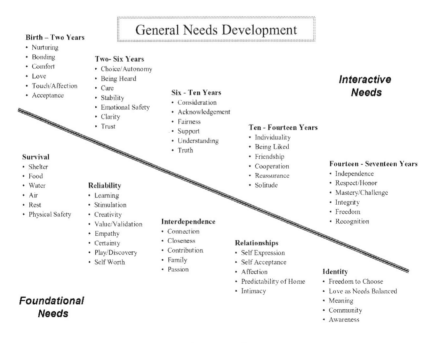

Used with permission. Corporate Culture Development © 2005

This book is published to expressly create a resource that can be used by people in the helping professions—by Counselors, Social Workers, Deputy Probation Officers, and Educators—so that more people in recovery from addiction get both clean and free and stay that way!

At the heart of every conversation I have with a probationer checking in and every question I ask is my need to be a positive contributor in that individual's present day life and in their future. The "system" for which I still enthusiastically work may label them "addicts," but I always see a person first. I see in every probationer and client as a human being who deserves a chance to redeem themselves, first for themselves and then for their family. A person can take back their power, get clean, and stay emotionally free. And that is what I think of as "The Final Step."

CHAPTER 1

DRUG ABUSE AND THE ABANDONED, WOUNDED, AND ORPHANED CHILD

"Narcotic Abuse, Divorce, and the Abandoned Child"

In my work as a Deputy Probation Officer, I discovered that the majority of my clients were wounded (emotional/physical), abandoned, or orphaned as children by their primary caretakers. And here is one important truth about our development as human beings: the needs of the child not being met turn into points of pathology or, in other words, "suffering" that is carried into the adult world. It may be emotional or physical pain and suffering, or over time it may be both together.

During the initial interview, as clients told their own stories, it became clear that these "adults" were examples of the Wounded Child and continued to hold onto the memories of the abuse, neglect, and other traumas they endured during their childhood. Emotional negligence by caregivers was the behavioral pattern my clients related to the most and it continued to be the main reason for their constant emotional pain as adults. All the emotional and abusive experiences of their childhood had a direct influence on their adult behavior.

The Orphan Child is another major characteristic or pattern that is reflected in the lives of my clients who believe, from an early age, that they are not part of their own family. Due to one parent's absence and the other's efforts to keep food on the table and a roof over their heads, the Orphan Child has to develop a sense of independence early in life in order to survive alone in the world. That they must survive alone in the world becomes a primary belief for them. The Orphan Child is usually unable to mature, both emotionally and socially, due to the feeling of denial by his family and will therefore seek acceptance in other places (e.g. gang affiliation, drug use with others). This type of client doesn't have much self-worth; they lack a grand vision or dreams or a sense of purpose in any situation. They will consequently sabotage anything positive in their world in order to manifest their life-diminishing belief system about themselves.

Working as a Deputy Probation Officer in the initial years of Proposition 36, I had daily opportunities to hear and see how past experiences that were emotionally overwhelming, hostile, unpredictable, unsafe, or depressing were directly related to excessive drug abuse by the client over the years. Whenever I brought up or discussed the client's family dynamics and how their caretakers responded to their needs as children, the majority of the clients stated that they had a great childhood. Their classic responses were "I love my parents" or "My parents provided food and shelter for me." I would then ask them if they felt they had the majority of their social/ emotional needs met as children. The majority did not understand the question.

These individuals did not understand what I meant when I used the term "meeting the needs" of the individual. "Did your caretakers meet any of your social/emotional needs?" I would then show them the "needs chart" so they could identify the types of needs their caretakers did or did not provide for them. Once the process was underway, I would ask them to be honest when making their choices. I observed that most of the clients had a difficult time realizing that the majority of their interpersonal needs were never met by their caretakers.

At this point in the dialogue, they'd begin to understand the truth and how their perception of their own childhood was not as they pictured or imagined. It was at this moment they began to understand how their drug use had become an important part of their lives and survival for so many years.

At this stage in the interview, an awakening and an understanding about their drug use began to occur. They'd begin to connect the dots for themselves!

And, once a client understands how their caretaker was unable to meet their social/emotional needs as children, they also begin to understand how their own present behavior is influenced by these harmful events of the past and why and how these events catalyzed their initial drug use that typically began during their early teens and continued for many years.

To a large degree most of our behavior is determined on an unconscious level. We, as individuals, begin to behave out of habit because certain psychological and social patterns develop over a long period of time—if never challenged. Below, I will discuss the "Three Phases of Waking Up."

Three States of Waking Up

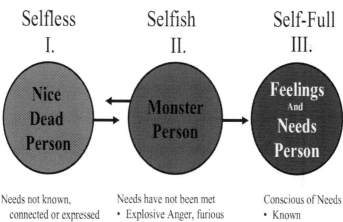

Selfless I.	Selfish II.	Self-Full III.
Nice Dead Person	Monster Person	Feelings And Needs Person

Needs not known, connected or expressed	Needs have not been met	Conscious of Needs
• Ignoring own needs	• Explosive Anger, furious	• Known
• Submit and Apologize	• Reactive	• Expressed
• Numb	• Illnesses / sickness /body aches	• Persistent action
	• Volatile	• Vibrant

© 2005 Corporate Culture Development

3

THREE PHASES OF WAKING UP

Phase 1: The initial phase of waking up is called "selfless." What this literally means is that the individual has no sense of self. He does not know what his needs are and he doesn't know how to meet those needs or how to ask for what he needs. So, basically, the person exists in the world as a "Nice Dead Person." A "nice dead person" usually navigates through life not understanding how to meet his needs or the needs of others. It is as if he operates in the world with an "unconscious" habit of behavior.

Phase 2: In the second phase the person becomes "selfish." The person, for the first time, has realized that his needs have not been met and he becomes furious and experiences explosive anger. He becomes reactive and in response his body becomes sick and he experiences aches and pains. To get those needs met, he now tries using aggressive tactics. The only ways he can communicate is by using language that will either make the other person submit or rebel. The individual will also use methods of judgment, criticism, blame, and shame to communicate with others. The primary result for this individual is that he wins the conversation or situation at any and all costs.

He is basically swinging the "needs" pendulum from one side to the other because he wants to get his needs met at the present time. However, he doesn't know how to get them met in a manner that is life serving to him or to those around him, so he uses the only language that he knows.

Another way to interpret this phase is to look at it as though a person is applying a new "belief" system about his way of thinking, behaving, and feeling in the world. This new way can be difficult to accept and change. Specific "behavioral" tactics were necessary to survive and navigate this "old" world. A new awareness that a majority of needs were never met by caregivers can be painful. Once a person understands and accepts how unmet needs have had an impact on his behavior and relationships with others, he will be ready for the final phase.

Phase 3: The third phase is what is called being "self-full." In this phase, the individual is aware of his needs and knows how to ask for them in a persistent manner. The individual begins to walk through life "unplugged" from situations around him. He is thoroughly aware of how he feels and how those feelings are connected to those needs. He now has empathy for himself and the ability to understand his feelings as experienced in real time and the particular needs that are connected to those feelings. Once this experience is obtained, the individual does not allow the situation to bury him emotionally. The individual understands where these feelings and needs come from and has the ability to convey that to others.

Michael S. Oden, M.A., Behavioral Specialist

A Client's Story: Abandoned Child

My client today is a forty-four-year-old black female who stated she has been using drugs since the age of eighteen. At the beginning of our conversation she told me that she wanted to change her ways because she was tired of going in and out of jail, prostituting herself, and not having any money or her own place to live. She had been living with her grandmother over the years.

I suggested that we have a dialogue to get to the core of her drug use so she could see how past events have affected her decision-making process. She was reluctant at first to discuss her past because she stated it was too painful. I explained that sometimes we need to go through the darkness to get to the light and that it may be emotionally painful; however, the reward for coming out the other end is becoming a person who finally has the answer to their problem.

She agreed to give it a go and began to explain how she was raised by her grandmother from a young age because her mother was on drugs and her father was never in the picture. The moment that changed her life forever occurred when she was seven years old: What she remembers was that she said something to her mother's friend that caused this person to become upset with her. This person walked over to my client and proceeded to remove her shoe and break my client's jaw. Her mother never confronted her friend about physically hurting her daughter.

Talking about this event sparked a curious thought that had never occurred to her before. She wondered why her mother never protected her or stood up for her. In time, she was taken away from her mother, who continued her excessive drug use and was in and out of jail for years.

During her adolescent years she lived with her grandmother. While attending school she remembers she was teased, bullied, and harassed by the other students.

She told me they made fun of her complexion because her skin is dark. They called her ugly and other names she didn't want to mention. She was able to graduate from high school but she never did anything with her life. She had bounced from job to job, man to man, and place to place for the last twenty-six years. She never established a career for herself and always believed she was not good enough to accomplish anything.

Another belief she created was that no one ever fought for her, especially her mother. She believed she deserved to be alone. I suggested to her that this was probably the root cause of her constant drug use. She gave me a look of confusion. She stated that she did not understand. I asked her the question, "When you take drugs what do you feel and where do you go?"

After some thought she stated, "It makes me forget about my problems and the emotional pain I've felt thinking about my mother abandoning me when I was a little girl."

So I then had her choose the "needs" that were not met by her caretakers. The needs she chose that she did not get from her caretakers were the following: nurturance, comfort, bonding, connection, support, reassurance, being heard, appreciation, love, family, validation, emotional safety, contribution, safety, protection, and security of home and family.

I then had her pick the feelings behind the needs that were not met by the caretaker. She chose the following: sad, lonely, helpless, gloom, grief, scared, terrified, nervous, mad, angry, bitter, confused, frustrated, tired, fatigued, uncomfortable, pained, hurt, embarrassed, and ashamed.

As she reviewed her responses she began to cry uncontrollably. She finally saw what she did not get from her caretakers, there in black and white, on paper and it struck her hard. I explained, "And this is why excessive drug use has become an important part of your life." I told her that she was not sick in the head and she didn't have a disease. I explained to her that she was emotionally wounded by her caretaker's inability to meet any of her social/emotional needs. And she had been doing the best she could for years.

After our discussion she shared that she felt relief for the first time in her life. It was as though a weight had been lifted that she had been carrying inside of her for a long time. I explained to her that all I was trying to do was make sense of her life and why she behaved the way she did. Now the challenge was to create a "value-shift" in her life where she could see "endless possibilities" as opposed to "impossibilities."

We still had some work to do about how her "past" had affected her; however, there was now an awareness and understanding that she'd never had before. Her new and conscious understanding would help in the healing process so she could develop the necessary tools to move forward with her life.

Then we talked about what needed to be done next and decided that since she didn't have to worry about covering her own basic living expenses of rent and food, thanks to her grandmother, she needed to enroll in a nearby community college and enjoy making some mistakes so she could learn from them.

I will wait until her next appointment to see how this new insight has affected her outlook on her life.

CHAPTER 2

WHERE IS MY FATHER?

"My mom worked two jobs and nobody was home."
As I began my search for the answer as to why these individuals began to use and/or abuse drugs/alcohol for an extended length of time and the emotion that was attached to their excessive drug use, I began to notice a pattern of the "absent father." I came to realize the detrimental impact an absent father had on their children, especially the boys, as I began to listen to my clients' childhood stories. These individuals longed for the attention and influence of their male role models. I can honestly say 85% to 95% of these individuals on Probation did not know their fathers, had never connected with their fathers, or were physically, psychologically, and/or emotionally abused by their father. They grew up often hearing phrases like: "You will never amount to anything." "Do you think you are better than me?" and "I wish you had never been born."

It was difficult for most of my clients, as adults, to admit that their own caretakers had actually said these types of cruel statements to them as children—and not just once but repeatedly. When exploring their relationships with their caretakers, especially their fathers, the majority of my clients never volunteered that the relationship with their fathers had been fragmented, or relayed the heartbreaking words that would send them down the road of confusion and self doubt. These were the kind of statements that were especially painful to hear growing up as a child.

Therefore, the initial question I asked my clients was what kind of relationship they had with their fathers as children, adolescents, teenagers, or young adults. Their first response was often: "I had a great relationship with my father," "I loved my father," or "He provided for me." The clients never mentioned anything negative or inappropriate about their fathers.

Knowing there was more to this question, I'd ask, "Do you remember any negative/positive comments your father said to you as a child or during your adolescent years?" or "How did your father interact with you when you were living with him as a child or young adult?"

Instinctively, the clients would respond by saying, "He was a great dad and I loved him." This is the part of the conversation where I began to discuss what social/emotional needs their fathers were clearly unable to fulfill. At this point, the clients would become emotionally uncomfortable because our dialogue challenged their reality of how they each believed their relationship with their father was.

The majority of my clients had a difficult time, initially, accepting the truth that their relationships with their fathers were not as they had envisioned. It was at this point of acceptance that the clients began to purge all the emotions they had been harboring inside themselves for years. This was the first time they realized they never had that emotional (father/son) connection they had believed to be true.

The image of their fathers would never be the same after experiencing the disappointment behind this truth. This was the moment the clients needed to admit to themselves that their fathers had their own social/emotional flaws and the clients had paid for those flaws. Understanding this truth would begin the shift to a new belief structure about themselves and the healing process could begin.

I really wanted my clients to have that understanding and awareness of how not having a socially/emotionally conscious father in their lives directly related to their behavior and the choices they made. I believed they needed to see the truth about how they envisioned their lives and what their reality was.

This process usually needed a few tissues to wipe away tears, but once they got through this portion of the session the remaining interview would be about healing their emotional wounds of the past. After this the "absent father syndrome" would no longer impact their present-day behavior. Will they have "emotional scars" from what their fathers did or did not give them? Absolutely.

However, once a client can have empathy for his father's behavior and see why his father was unable to be present and meet his social/emotional needs, he can begin the deep and liberating healing process.

Fatherless Children

Plenty of research has been done on the effects of being raised in a single-parent family and sadly, the trend of fatherlessness is on the rise. Fatherless children are at a disadvantage and are more likely than children raised in two-parent families to do poorly in school, have emotional and behavioral problems, become teenage parents, and have poverty-level incomes as adults. According to U.S. Census Bureau information pertaining to America's Families and Living Arrangements released on the Internet in November 2012:

- 25% of families with children (under age eighteen) were maintained by mothers.
- 32% of the 35 million families with children (under age eighteen) were maintained by one parent
- 79% of single-parent families were mother-only families and
- 21% were father-only families.
- 60% of children born during the 1990s spent a significant portion of their childhood in a home without their biological father.

(Source: http://www.census.gov/hhes/families/data/cps2012.html)

"You're Pushing My Buttons!!!"

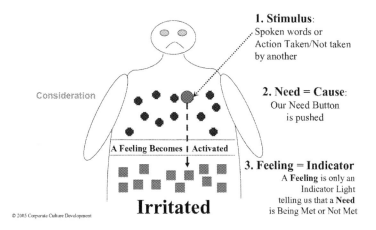

1. Stimulus:
Spoken words or
Action Taken/Not taken
by another

2. Need = Cause:
Our Need Button
is pushed

3. Feeling = Indicator
A **Feeling** is only an
Indicator Light
telling us that a **Need**
is Being Met or Not Met

Consideration

A Feeling Becomes Activated

Irritated

© 2005 Corporate Culture Development

I Push My Buttons From the Inside

This graph displays the various needs/feelings buttons we as "human beings" have within us. So, when a need is being met or not met, a feeling arises. A feeling is only an "indicator light" that a "need" is being met or not met.

Here is a client story to illustrate the previous illustration. This particular client was terrified when his father came home drunk, because in a drunken rage, his father would begin to beat his mother. This client had a need for emotional safety, physical safety, comfort, peace, and security of home and family. It was apparent his social/emotional needs were not being met every time this scenario occurred. Now the emotions (feelings) that arise out of his lack of specific needs being met can vary. This client can have the emotions of being scared, terrified, nervous, frightened, fatigued, tired, frustrated, uneasy, and worried to name a few; all due to a certain amount of needs not being met at that particular time.

Notice all of the "need buttons" that were pushed that caused this client to feel those particular emotions. Now if we have certain social/emotional needs that will not be met this creates specific negative emotions. And, if we have somewhere between ten to fifteen unmet needs, the client will likely become overwhelmed, depressed, or hostile to the situation. This is where most people will resort to an artificial means (i.e. drug use) to diminish their anxiety triggered by the event.

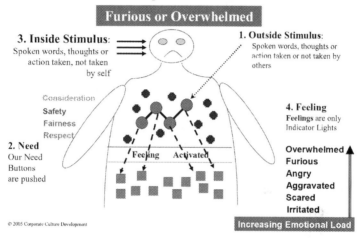

"That Person Pushes My Buttons" Plus "I Push My Own Buttons"

For example, on 9/11/09, I had a fifty-one-year-old Black male who was friends with the founders of the Bloods and Crips, Tookie and a Mr. Washington. When discussing his drug use through the late 1970s and into the 80s, he also mentioned that he had been a young musician who experimented with cocaine and women on a constant basis and that all of his peers had done it. The client also mentioned that he didn't use drugs until he was seventeen or eighteen years of age when he began traveling with his band as a drummer.

When I asked him where his father was in his life, he mentioned that he had a great relationship with his father. His father had provided a stable home environment and he was taken care of due to his father working. As the client continued to discuss his childhood, I interrupted him and asked him if he had connected with his father on a daily basis then why the drug use over the years? Why did he need to use drugs? What was the "need" that was being met by the drugs? He sat back in the chair and, after contemplating a minute, gave me a look of a little boy who had relinquished the truth about his father. He stated that he really didn't see his father because he worked long hours and that he didn't see his mother because she worked nights.

It was at this point of awareness I began to inform the client of the social/emotional needs that his caretakers were unable to meet due to their working long hours or hours that conflicted with spending time with the client as a young boy.

For the first time in his life, the client stated that he didn't have the connection he believed he'd had with his caretakers, especially his father. The client was taken back by this new discovery and stated he was amazed by this new piece of information. He couldn't believe how that piece of information could have such an impact on him at that moment. This information also made sense as to why he felt the need to have so many one-night stands with women over the years. I mentioned to him that each event was a way to get his need met for validation and connection. I mentioned to him that it's possible that each one-night stand may have been him trying to make up for what his caretakers were unable to give him.

Again, he stopped and stared into space. At the end of our conversation, the client stated he now had a different outlook about his drug use and how the underlying events of the past directly correlated to his drug use. He mentioned that he would not look at drug use in the same way.

The previous story is another example of what I have encountered many times over the years. It is again the story of a child who wanted to believe that his caretakers met his social/emotional needs and the reality of what truly transpired with the father/son dynamics and the needs that were never met.

The Effects of Fatherlessness (based on U.S. Data)

BEHAVIORAL DISORDERS/RUNAWAYS/HIGH SCHOOL
DROPOUTS/CHEMICAL ABUSERS/SUICIDE

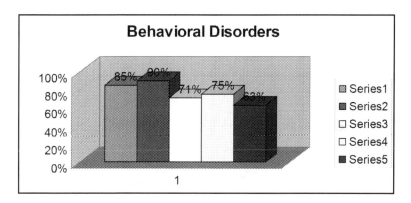

- 85% of all children that exhibit behavioral disorders come from fatherless homes (Source: Center for Disease Control)
- 90% of all homeless and runaway children are from fatherless homes (Source: U.S. D.H.H.S., Bureau of the Census)
- 71% of all high school dropouts come from fatherless homes (Source: National Principals Association Report on the State of High Schools.)
- 75% of all adolescent patients in chemical abuse centers come from fatherless homes (Source: Rainbows for all God's Children.)
- 63% of youth suicides are from fatherless homes

(Source: U.S. D.H.H.S., Bureau of the Census)

JUVENILE DELINQUENCY/ CRIME/ GANGS

- 80% of rapists motivated with displaced anger come from fatherless homes (Source: Criminal Justice & Behavior, Vol. 14, p. 403-26, 1978)
- 70% of juveniles in state-operated institutions come from fatherless homes (Source: U.S. Dept. of Justice, Special Report, Sept 1988)

How do these statistics translate? Children from fatherless homes are:

- 5 times more likely to commit suicide.
- 32 times more likely to run away.
- 20 times more likely to have behavioral disorders.
- 14 times more likely to commit rape
- 9 times more likely to drop out of high school.
- 10 times more likely to abuse chemical substances.
- 9 times more likely to end up in a state-operated institution.
- 20 times more likely to end up in prison.

Criminal behavior experts and social scientists are finding intriguing evidence that the epidemic of youth violence and gangs is related to the breakdown of the two-parent family. "New Evidence That Quayle Was Right: Young Offenders Tell What Went Wrong at Home" San Francisco Chronicle (12/9/94).

TEENAGE PREGNANCY

"Daughters of single parents are 53% more likely to marry as teenagers, 164% more likely to have a premarital birth, and 92% more likely to dissolve their own marriages. All these intergenerational consequences of single motherhood increase the likelihood of chronic welfare dependency." Barbara Dafoe Whitehead, Atlantic Monthly (April 1993).

CHILD ABUSE

The U.S. Department of Health and Human Services states that there were more than one million documented child abuse cases in 1990. In 1983, it found that 60% of perpetrators were women with sole custody. Shared parenting can significantly reduce the stress associated with sole custody and reduce the isolation of children in abusive situations by allowing both parents to monitor the children's health and welfare and to protect them.

(Source: http://www.fclu.org/parentless-statistics/)

"My Mother worked two jobs!" the equation

If I had to create an equation that was the underlying theme for my clients and explain how this equation was relative to their life-diminishing behavior (e.g. Drug use, high school dropout, abusive relationships, child abandonment, etc.) it would look like this: Absent Father (death, state prison, working long hours, running the streets) plus Overworked/Stressed Mother (making ends meet by working two jobs, caring for multiple siblings, emotionally overwhelmed, not receiving any type of support) equals: No caretaker at home.

A child with no caretaker to create boundaries or to meet their social/emotional needs creates a child whose need for freedom and choice becomes his reality as an adolescent. This lack of influence by the caretaker creates an atmosphere of limitless freedom, hence the anti-social behavior of the individual which creates the last segment of the formula: life-diminishing behavior (bullying, gang activity, drug dependency, teenage pregnancy, criminal activity, hostile/violent relationships) which leads to state prison, county jail, or death.

Absent Father + <u>Overworked/stressed mother</u> = *Nobody home* + ***life diminishing behavior*** = state prison, drug abuse, gangs, criminal behavior, death.

I cannot tell you how many times I heard a client tell me that there wasn't anyone home to watch over them when they came home from school. Therefore, that unsupervised home life allowed them to behave in a manner that would push their social/emotional limits. The lack of boundaries and connection with the caretaker is the recipe for them to commit crimes, get arrested, use drugs, ditch school, and join a gang if it was appropriate.

Not only had the father disappeared, but the mother was usually too tired to connect with the child in anyway due to the demands of her job. With that reality, the child was usually left to fend for himself, which usually meant finding connection, purpose, and meaning elsewhere (gangs, drug use) since he couldn't get his interpersonal needs met by the caretaker.

A Client's Story: The three o'clock deadline

Today I had a client that I went into depth with regarding her drug use. Here is her story.

Maria was a thirty-four-year-old Hispanic divorced mother of three daughters, ages seventeen, eighteen, and nineteen. When I initially asked her how she got into this predicament she stated that she was arrested for possession. So I asked her why she was using in the first place. She stated that when situations become too difficult for her to handle she would relapse. So, I decided to go back in time to see where this response to anxiety originated.

After several minutes of discussing her childhood experiences she stated that at the age of seven, as the oldest, she was responsible for cleaning the house and preparing the food so her mother could cook when she returned from work.

After more discussion, she also stated that if the house wasn't clean and the food was not prepared for cooking, her mother would beat her with an electric cord or other objects. So, from the age of seven to the age of eighteen, my client was under constant pressure to perform the way her mother had trained her, and if she didn't she would suffer the consequences. My client stated that she became frightened when three o'clock approached because she wanted to make sure everything was in order as her mother instructed. It is apparent that my client did not receive many life serving social/emotional needs from her caretakers that a child requires to have a healthy view of herself, her immediate surroundings, and the world around her.

I directed my client to pick out what needs she believed she didn't get from her mother. Here were her choices: nurturance, physical affection, tenderness, comfort, bonding, respect, connection, support, trust, being heard, appreciation, love, affection, contribution, emotional safety, sharing, validation, family, self-expression, growth, goals, play, humor, stimulation, pleasure, safety, protection, and security of home and family. As she was making her choices she began to cry because she realized for the first time in her life what she hadn't gotten from the people she wanted it from the most. It was apparent that her needs not being met attributed to how she viewed herself and those around her. She always believed she had to prove herself to others.

When discussing her father, she mentioned that he worked a lot and didn't spend much time with the children. Plus, he was not aware of the beatings from the mother. Needless to say, she didn't get many needs from her father due to his work schedule.

So I asked her how her past showed up in her present and her thoughts for the future[. She told me her story. She told me her first husband, after two years of marriage, began to verbally and physically abuse her. She stated that she put up with it for ten years because her father told her to stay with her man, even during the difficult times. She finally realized that she had had enough and got out of the marriage.

Drug use became prevalent during the marriage and remained so as of today. We discovered that her drug use allowed her a certain emotional freedom and independence (because she never could make her own choices). We discovered that everything around her had to be spotless because if it wasn't she would believe herself to be worthless. This was due to her mother teaching her that self-worth was tied into how clean the house was. So, she manifests that belief system into her present life. She stated to me that when situations become overwhelming or when she is unable to take control of a situation, she relapses. She believes she is a failure because she didn't take care of the matter at hand. This goes back to how she was raised by her mother.

So, it is safe to say that her drug use is attributed to whether she has control of her life and those individuals in it. If she sees that she is losing control or situations are not going like she wants them to go, she will relapse.

FYI: Today, she cleans houses for a living. I actually laughed when she told me. I told her, "Gee, I wonder why." She stated that she has to keep moving because she's been moving since she was seven years old by constantly cleaning. We also discussed her not having a childhood. She totally agreed, "I didn't know what it was like to just have fun and be silly. I was always on guard with my mother." She did mention that she did guide her children into activities that they were interested in doing and that she had a great time participating in their activities to make up for never having had any fun as a child herself.

At the end of our conversation I decided to give her a project. Since she needs to have everything neat and tidy at her home I told her to not make up the bed once a week and be comfortable with being uncomfortable about the messy bed. I wanted her to experience what life is like when there is a piece of dust on the floor, the dishes are in the sink, or the bed isn't made. I want her to come back next month and tell me how she did with the unmade bed. Basically, I want her to experience the certain needs she never had as a child such as emotional safety, choice, self-worth, and physical safety. I also want to see how she will handle overwhelming situations without using drugs.

When Maria returned the following month I asked her how her experiment had gone. She shared that she had tried hard not to clean the house obsessively and had managed to skip making her bed once a week. Although difficult at first it became easier as the weeks went by. Knowing she wasn't being judged by her mother helped. She wasn't being punished for not making her bed nor was she punishing herself. I was confident now that her life would be different; and her need for drugs in response to overwhelming situations was no longer an obstacle.

CHAPTER 3

MAKING SENSE OF THE CRIMINAL THINKING STYLES

Thinking styles and the importance of completing the instructional system

How a person thinks by default and under stress became an important detail in getting to understand how my clients viewed the world as they tried to make sense of it and their role in it. And, as I have stated before, I wanted to do more than just supervise them as in most cases they reported to me monthly. I wanted to know how their perception or "skew" of their surroundings affected their decision making process. My larger goal was to see them succeed in completing their grant of probation and help them see a future full of potential for themselves and their families.

I am thankful that I met William Stierle who introduced me to the Whole Brain Thinking® Model Instrument and with whom I began a mentoring relationship that continues to introduce me to some extraordinary communication tools and strategies.

Early in my career as a Deputy Probation Officer, I was introduced to several resources that would dramatically improve communication and understanding between myself and my clients. One of those resources is known as the Whole Brain Thinking® Model. This model for understanding how people think, react, interact, learn, and communicate with others was developed by William "Ned" Herrmann while working in a corporate environment in the 1980s. Like many things developed to improve commercial ventures, it too has been creatively and successfully applied to other fields and industries. I saw in this "tool" and this "instrument for assessment" as a way to get clearer insight about why particular thinking and communication preferences of the clients would never materialize because "during childhood" their caretaker did not allow the clients to express that part of their thinking.

The Whole Brain Thinking® Model identifies four different modes of thinking. We, as individuals, have certain thinking and communication preferences as well as our default mode when reacting to stressful events. We also have secondary modes that we can develop with effort. What I find interesting and key to recovery is how a person uses these different styles to navigate the world and, specifically, their own inner world.

In his Whole Brain Thinking® Model, Herrmann identifies four different modes of thinking:

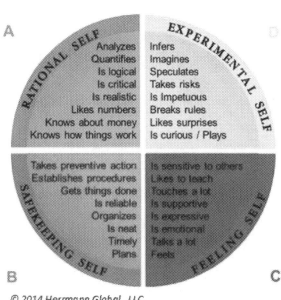

© 2014 Herrmann Global, LLC.

The four-color, four-quadrant graphic and Whole Brain® are registered trademarks of Herrmann Global, LLC. © 2014 Herrmann Global, LLC.

Here are the preferences of the four thinking styles:

■A. Analytical thinking
Key words: logical, factual, critical, technical, quantitative. Preferred activities: collecting data for analysis; understanding how things work; judging ideas based on facts, criteria, and logical reasoning.

■B. Sequential thinking
Key words: safekeeping, structured, organized complexity, detailed, planned. Preferred activities: following directions, detail oriented work, step-by-step problem solving, organization, implementation.

■C. Interpersonal thinking
Key words: kinesthetic, emotional, spiritual, sensory, feeling. Preferred activities: group interaction, listening to and expressing ideas, looking for personal meaning, seeking sensory input.

■D. Imaginative thinking
Key words: Visual, holistic, intuitive, innovative, conceptual. Preferred activities: Looking at the big picture, taking initiative, challenging assumptions, visualizing, metaphoric thinking, creative problem solving, long term thinking.

(Source:http://dictionary.sensagent.com/
herrmann+brain+dominance+instrument/en-en/)

Why is understanding a person's thinking style important?
According to the Whole Brain Thinking® Model Instrument (HBDI®) every person has a preferential thinking style but it is possible to develop the ability to use the other thinking styles. Through my research, I discovered that a large percentage of my clients' preferential thinking styles were shut down early in life because of the major influence of parental beliefs that

were passed on or by the major influence of environmental circumstances that could not be controlled.

Imagine that another thinking style is imposed on a person by a major influence in that person's life; a style that runs counter to their natural thinking tendencies. In this scenario, the client potentially becomes frustrated, angry, and possibly hostile when they are unable to use their preferential thinking style.

What Frustrates Each Quadrant of the Whole Brain® Model

A	D
❏ Inarticulate, 'off the track' communication ❏ Excessive 'chatter' ❏ Vague, ambiguous approaches or instructions ❏ Illogical comments ❏ Inefficient use of time ❏ Lack of facts or data ❏ Inappropriate informality ❏ Overt sharing of personal feelings ❏ Fear of challenge or debate ❏ Impression of not knowing the 'right' answer	❏ Repetition ❏ Too slow paced ❏ 'Playing it safe' or 'by the book' ❏ Overtly structured, predictable ❏ Absence of humor and fun ❏ Lack of flexibility, too rigid ❏ Inability to get concepts or metaphors ❏ Drowning in detail ❏ Too many numbers ❏ Dry, boring topic or style
❏ Unknown or absence of a clear agenda ❏ Disorganized ❏ Hopping around from subject to subject ❏ Too many ideas at once ❏ Unpredictable ❏ Too fast paced ❏ Unclear instructions or language ❏ Too much beating around the bush ❏ Incomplete sentences ❏ Lack of closure	❏ Lack of interaction ❏ No eye contact ❏ Impersonal approach or examples ❏ Dry or 'cold' un-enthusiastic interaction ❏ Insensitive comments ❏ No time for personal sharing ❏ All data, no nonsense ❏ Lack of respect for feelings ❏ Overly direct or brusque dialogue ❏ Critical
B	C

The four-color, four-quadrant graphic and Whole Brain® are registered trademarks of Herrmann Global, LLC.
© 2014 Herrmann Global , LLC

For example, in many cases my Hispanic clients were creative and imaginative and would, therefore, seek jobs that required these types of skills. However, there were cultural/generational differences between the client and their parent who had come over to America by foot. The belief system of the parent influenced what belief system they preferred to instill in their children. Basically, they wanted their child to *also* choose work that created a tangible product; to take a job that was safekeeping and reliable. At the end of the day, the client needed to show that something was created or the caretaker didn't believe it was an actual job or work worth valuing. Gardening and construction were encouraged but being an artist or musician was not acceptable.

For these clients, I had to clarify how their caretakers viewed the world in a safekeeping practical manner. My clients, exposed to American culture when they were young, experienced the world where their strongest preference guided them into their career of choice. This basic explanation gave the client the understanding and clarity they needed in regards to how their parents viewed the world as opposed to how the client viewed the world. But giving the client understanding of this difference did not always mean the client proceeded to do what he preferred.

The most common outcome was that their cultural ties had more influence over their preference and, therefore, the client continued to involve themselves in work that would never fit their preference. However, it would meet the financial needs their caretakers required.

This is one example of how Whole Brain Thinking® Model increased my ability to be effective when discussing a client's history, their present circumstances, and their goals. I met the client where they were at, attempting to speak to them in a language they could hear, assimilate, and react to safely. I did not presume that they would adapt to my chosen thinking style. I adapted to theirs for the sake of teaching them that there were other ways of looking at their reality. I attribute the quick rapport I had with Probation clients to my use of tools like NVC and Whole Brain Thinking® Model.

I believe it is important to know the categories/preferences of a person who is part of the criminal justice system and understand how they will interact with the person they are supervised by (who is part of the law enforcement system). Typically, a person in law enforcement has a preference for gathering facts, solving problems logically, establishing procedures, and taking preventive action. Whereas the criminal element usually recognizes new possibilities, challenges established policies, and is clearly willing to take risks. And, ideally, a client and Probation Officer can work together to understand where each is coming from.

Following the requirements of probation is a "blue and green oriented task" and falls into the Analytical and Sequential Thinking Quadrants. Probation Officers are in charge of seeing that clients follow and complete their grant of probation. Often though, clients fall into the Imaginative and Interpersonal Thinking Quadrants and are inclined to be "red and yellow" as they are looking for new ways to take risks, bend rules, and experiment. Something got them in deep trouble in the first place. It is possible to get a client on board with the idea of completing their "grant of probation" if you are communicating with them in a way that relates to their thinking style and in a language they can process.

Prior to 2003, when I was introduced to the HBDI® model by William Stierle, I was already effective in my role as a Deputy Probation Officer thanks to my understanding and integration of NVC. Where the use of NVC was primary in my work with all my clients, the knowledge of Whole Brain Thinking® Model made working with clients, especially those who were angry at their parents, go more smoothly. HBDI® was instrumental as a supporting resource to increase clarity around parent-child thinking styles and the belief system of the parents that often clashed with the self-image of the client.

What is the bottom line concerning the Whole Brain Thinking® Model as I employ it in my counseling work?

1. Knowing what kind of communication style a person prefers allows for asking the right kinds of questions.
2. Asking questions in the right style makes a person more responsive.
3. Knowing a person's preferred language style allows us to stop using derogatory phrases about their style of communication.

There is more than one way for individuals to communicate and live with each other in a peaceful and supportive way—allowing other people also to be themselves. There have been unfortunate—even devastating—consequences to a rigid emphasis on left oriented Analytical and Sequential thinking as superior to Imaginative and Interpersonal or right oriented thinking.

Well-meaning parents unknowingly constrict their children by failing to recognize and honor right-oriented as well as left-oriented gifts with respect to education and career choices.

1. Well-intentioned teachers take their students down the wrong learning path because they don't know how to discern and use the preferred learning style of each student.

2. Well-intentioned professionals (therapist, counselors, social workers, Probation Officers) insist upon filtering a client through their preferred modes of communication to get their work done and their case notes completed.

A Client's Story: "I never had freedom"

A twenty-eight-year-old black female reported to my office with her nine-year-old nephew. Curious as to how and why she was on Probation, I asked how she came upon her Proposition 36 situation. She stated that she was caught using various drugs. Again, I asked why she would be using drugs in the first place. Her response was, "Because I wanted to." I said, "I understand that. Why did you want to?"

She answered again by saying, "Because it made me feel better." I responded by saying, "Better than what?" I could tell at this point that she was getting frustrated by my continued questioning, so I explained to her that my reasoning for delving into her life was to discover the "why" of her drug use so she could stop. I asked her to tell me when she began using drugs. She stated that she started when she was a teenager. I asked what was going on during her teenage years that influenced her drug use. She stated that she had to attend church three to four times a week, she wasn't allowed to have friends, and she wasn't allowed to explore the world as a teenager. I asked her if she would describe her parents as "running a strict household?"

Her face lit up and she stated, "Yes, my parents were very strict." I then asked her, "So, could your drug use be attributed to your need for choice, freedom, and individuality?" "Yes," she said. She stated that she never got to do anything different and felt as if she were trapped in her own house. She mentioned that throughout her teenage years she continued to rebel against the rules of the house, which is why she didn't complete her high school education. It was after she left the house that the drug use became more prevalent because she was not used not having any rules to follow and she did what most people do in her situation: she took advantage of the freedom she never had as a child. So, from the age of eighteen to twenty-eight her life began to spiral out of control. She was in and out of jail for various crimes and going nowhere fast.

Today, she lives with her mother. She is back where she started as a child. During our conversation, she did get a better understanding and awareness as to why she behaved in the manner she did. In other words, how she got her need for choice, self-expression, respect, and self-empowerment met by using narcotics and participating in anti-social behavior. She stated that all she ever wanted was for her parents to listen to what she had to say, offer some bonding and comfort and some understanding. Now that she has an understanding she can make the necessary adjustments regarding what she wants to do with her life, such as complete her high school education.

CHAPTER 4

PHYSICAL ABUSE AND SEXUAL ABUSE

"Hide the Shame": Verbal, Emotional, Physical, and Sexual Abuse

There were clients who decided I would be the first person they would tell their story to; they chose to tell me the truth about why they used drugs for such a long period of time. I would ask them when their drug use began and why. I made it my practice to be an active listener, respectful in responding to whatever they shared with me, and I opted to go the candid route with questions from the first meeting.

It was at this juncture in the interviews that I would get information I was not anticipating from the client. For those clients who had an "aha" experience, the initial response would vary from being a loud, gut-wrenching roar and a fetal cry like a baby. For the majority of these clients, I was the first person they had ever trusted enough to tell about their sexual abuse experience. This was the initial point during the interview that their healing process would begin. Such was the case for a client named Sergio

The first time I met Sergio, he appeared nervous, tentative, and avoided eye contact when I spoke to him. As a Proposition 36 Probation client, he wasn't going to jail for his criminal offense of illegal drug possession if he were to complete his court ordered drug treatment obligation and his grant of probation. I assured Sergio that I was not the type of supervising officer that would make his life more uncomfortable. I truly wanted to help him understand why he'd put himself in the position he was in so that he might avoid relapsing, potential jail time, and most importantly he'd become emotionally free. After several minutes of conversation Sergio stated that he wanted to share a fifteen-year-old secret he had never told anyone. He had been carrying this secret inside himself since he was nine years old. Before he said anything further, I told him that what he shared with me might be the key to understanding his past behaviors, why he became a gang member, and his constant use of illicit drugs.

Sergio took a deep breath, raised his head, and looked directly into my eyes. He calmly stated that he had been sexually abused between the ages of nine and eleven by his aunt. His mother, who worked full-time, had asked her sister for help with after school childcare. He said that his aunt would give him alcohol (Jack Daniels on the rocks) so that he would be incoherent and then she would have sex with him. As a child, Sergio didn't really know what was happening to him, so he tried to block out each experience as it occurred. This behavior came to a stop when his mother considered him old enough to not need a babysitter after school. As a child, Sergio never spoke up—he never spoke of this abuse till that first day in my office.

Sergio stated that he was too afraid to say anything to his parents because he was too embarrassed and ashamed. As he entered adolescence Sergio became angry, hostile, and rebellious. He explained that he had all these pent-up emotions and did not know what to do with them. As a teenager, he joined a gang where he experienced some stability, only to find himself in and out of juvenile hall. As a young adult, he buried his emotional pain by consuming more drugs and getting arrested multiple times for possession of a narcotic substance, which caused him to spend time in county jail as well as in state prison. Sergio would spend most of his life coping with the constant presence of shame. He didn't realize that keeping the secret of this abuse in childhood was causing him more damage the older he became. He was but one client of many with a similar story.

Understanding the Origin of Shame
For many of my clients using alcohol, methamphetamine, heroin, cocaine, etc. were all that was needed to numb the fear, emotional pain, and childhood memory of an encounter with a sexual predator. As a younger

child, they were vulnerable to the size of the trusted individual who violated them. Fighting back and winning was seldom a viable option.

These particular clients were sexually abused by someone they knew personally, someone they trusted, and someone who was supposed to protect and care for them. It was their own mother, father, babysitter, stepmother, stepfather, neighbor, family friend, or relative. Unfortunately, each client held on to an image of helplessness for many years, never confiding in anyone about what was manifesting emotionally inside them. The emotional, social, and behavioral reaction by each client being sexually abused was similar in nature; they all survived by hiding their shame. These clients essentially lost their ability to trust. They were afraid to get close to anyone for fear of having no control in any situation and being abused again. They could not manage close relationships due to trust issues, which affected past and present relationships.

Once we established the origin of their great emotional pain, we could explore how these traumatic events were the basis for their drug use. When they confided in me about what happened I usually responded, "Now we know the source of your drug problem." Initially, they gave me a puzzled look as if I had said something strange. They would ask me, "What do you mean, 'there's my drug problem'?"

My next questions were: "When you began to consume drugs, where did the experience take you?" "What are the benefits of using drugs, excessively?" The usual response was: "It made me forget my problems." "It made me do things I wouldn't normally do if I was sober." "It got me put in jail." "It messed up my life." "I don't really know because no one ever asked me that question before."

It appeared I needed to be clearer in my question and answer sessions. So, I would try another angle. "Why did you need to use artificial chemicals to alter your state of mind and body?" Or if a more direct approach was needed I would ask, "Why did you need to escape in the first place?" "What events occurred in your life that caused you pain, fear, or suffering?"

After some thought, they began to understand where I was going. Another challenging question I would often ask was, "What's in your 'real world' that you don't want to face?" or "What traumatic events or what individual are you running away from?"

Then they began to see the unpleasant but necessary journey we were going to take. As they began to name the unfortunate events of their past they did not want to deal with, they also realized that I was not looking at their drug use as the problem but the events that were directly related to their drug use. These clients came to the realization that I was not judging them, that I actually wanted to help them. Because of their newfound trust in me, they were willing to take the painful journey of understanding their past trauma so they could let go of their shame and, therefore, their healing could begin.

The next chart involves what people actually observe and what they interpret through their observation. In the Cycle of Shame, a person is determined to "control" and not repeat destructive behavior they are engaged in. They will say, "I will never do that again" but they do because they are dependent on the high they get from the destructive behavior that alleviates their white-knuckled anxiety. Their objective is to survive another day. Eventually they "release" the control and relapse into old behavior. Now they say, "How could I have done that again?" Then comes the state to "submit" where they shame themselves for what they did. The internal message is, "I am sorry. What have I done?" Lastly, they will "rebel" against their new (changing) beliefs. The rebel shows up in their mind and says, "Just this once." "I can do what I want!" "This is my life!" And the cycle repeats until the work to break it is done.

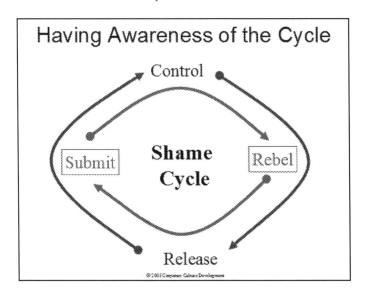

Control: I will never do that again.

Release: How could I have done that again?

Submit: I am sorry. What is wrong with me?

Rebel: Just this once. Because this is my life.

The highest form of intelligence is when a person can observe activity without evaluation, judgment, criticism, blame, or shame. The person is merely expressing what he sees with no additives. When I could get my clients to understand the social/emotional needs that were being met by their drug use they could begin to empathize with the cause of the drug use, be it parents, caregivers, their situation, or a traumatic experience. They could also begin to unload and release the shameful identity they had carried with them.

As I got to know my clients and listened to their stories of suffering, neglect, and abuse, I came to realize that the majority of my clients carried a lot of shame about themselves. The belief system that they developed in childhood was that they were the problem, hence they were abandoned, abused, and neglected by their caretaker. They created the belief that "I could have been a better child." In other words, it was their fault that their father never showed up; therefore, they must have done something wrong in order for him not to come back or, maybe, they didn't do enough to keep him from leaving.

It is apparent that the majority of my clients grew up in dysfunctional families that sent and received messages of unrelenting shame on a daily basis. As children, they had normal social/emotional needs and desires such as being held, accepted, validated, emotionally safe, given the opportunity to have choice, and asked questions about the world around them. If given the opportunity by their caretakers, all children will be allowed to push boundaries and establish their own identities. Unfortunately, the majority of these social/emotional needs often go unmet in dysfunctional families.

What is disturbing is that my clients who were raised in dysfunctional families were often subjected to various forms of punishment, guilt, blame, or shame because they had specific needs that were unable to be met by their caretakers. Imagine being punished for asking for help on homework—not realizing the adult you are asking can't read. Instead he yells at you and shames you for being so stupid that you can't do it on your own.

Because of their childhood upbringings, my clients have developed their own identities and feelings about themselves according to the way their caretakers responded to their social/emotional needs. After years of caretaker abuse and neglect, the feelings of toxic family shame are stored in the unconscious, where the interpretation of those messages continue to have an impact on how they navigate in the world. Once feelings of shame have been triggered, the client will move into a cycle of shame in which he will lock on to a particular behavior for survival, to protect himself from being further shamed.

Clients who come from this emotionally fragmented background will become defensive, argumentative, or will withdraw from others. All of these protective behaviors perpetuate the shame cycle. Unfortunately, a family environment in which shame plays a dominant role teaches a child to live by the following rules:

1. Feeling badly about yourself.
2. Dissatisfaction from your assessment of a decrease in stature.
3. Disapproving of your own actions or accomplishments.
4. Failure to meet your own standard of behavior.
5. Absence or deficiency of self-love. [Gil]
6. Feeling inferior.
7. Believing you are a bad person.
8. Loss of honor.
9. Blaming yourself for making mistakes.
10. Knowing you did wrong when it was possible to do right.
11. Not meeting your responsibility to yourself.

(Source: http://www.emotionalcompetency.com/emotion.htm)

From time to time even the best of caretakers/parents can be unpredictable and unreliable. In the eyes of children who have experienced abuse, the need for physical and emotional survival dictates that it's much safer to be attached to things like money, alcohol, sex, pornography, work, material goods, or food. Shame is also directly correlated to addiction, depression, violence, bullying, aggression, suicide, and eating disorders.

Some would say that there is a degree of justifiable shame. Justifiable shame is considered a healthy emotion because shame in small doses can curb an unwanted behavior; however, unjustifiable shame can be converted to a state of being. To have shame as an identity is to believe that one's being is imperfect, that one is impaired or damaged as a human being. Once shame becomes one's identity, shame becomes a toxic and dehumanizing (life-destroying) force that will dramatically impact how a person sees themselves. My intent as a human being, in a counseling role or otherwise, is *always* to empower, not to shame people.

Over the years, in discussing a client's past traumatic experiences and the impact on their beliefs and self-image, I always wondered if my clients ever felt any guilt about their criminal behavior. I can honestly say my client's did take responsibility for any destructive behavior or wrongdoing they participated in over the years such as: criminal activity, neglecting or abandoning their own children, not getting a GED, and drug dependency. Consistently, a client's guilt surfaced when we succeeded through dialogue in bringing their past behaviors, thoughts, and feelings to the surface. Then they could see how their decisions impacted the quality of their life, the lives of their families, and the lives of their children. For the majority of my clients, they never understood the social/emotional impact of not having a responsible male adult in their life because they never had it, so they didn't even know what that "father figure" looked like.

A Client's Story: "He beat my mother…"

A thirty-six-year-old Hispanic male came into my office for the usual monthly enrollment protocol. When he sat down I asked him how he got into this predicament, meaning how did he get arrested for drug possession. He mentioned that he was coming home from a party with his boys and was stopped by the police who found narcotics on his person. So, I asked him what drugs he had on him, he said he had marijuana. I asked him how long he had been consuming marijuana. He stated that he had been smoking weed every day since he was thirteen years old. I then informed him that he had been smoking weed for twenty-three years of his life.

He gave me a blank stare as he processed my last statement. I asked him why he thought he'd been smoking for such a long period of time. He stated that he just wanted to gain acceptance from his friends. Now I was thinking that some tragic event must have happened around the age of thirteen. I believed there had to be more to the story then only gaining acceptance from a group of people. So, I went deeper with my questioning. I asked him the one question most of my clients are not prepared to see the truth in and that is, "What was going on at home?" "What was your home life like?" "How did you get along with your father?" He gave me this strange stare. He paused for a moment and blurted out, "I used to watch my father come home drunk and beat my mother when I was a small child." Then a few moments later he added that "he and his brother used to wet their pants when his father would walk through the front door due to the terror they experienced." I threw my hands up and stated, "Now you have the answer as to why you used marijuana consistently for the past twenty-three years."

I explained to him that gaining "acceptance" was not the primary reason for using weed, it was secondary. The primary reason was to meet his need for emotional safety due to the feeling of fear, shock, and helplessness he experienced when his father physically abused his mother during his formative years. The client gave me a look and said that I was correct. I stated to him that, "I bet you didn't finish high school." He said, "How did you know?" I informed him that he was too distracted from his domestic problems to concentrate in school and, therefore, probably ditched school. He said it was true. I informed him that ditching school and running away for weeks at a time was the only way he could handle all the chaos and emotional pressure. The client stated that our conversation began to make sense of his past behavior and that he was getting a better understanding as to why he thought, felt, and behaved the way he did.

I explained to him that "The best thing you received out of this conversation is that you now understand the correlation between the trauma you experienced at home for many years and the amount of narcotics you consumed over the years."

To date, the client has stated that his father does not drink anymore and doesn't physically abuse his mother. However, he did state that his father is still angry and unable to connect or bond with him.

I explained to the client that the next project for him was to have "empathy" for this father and mother. I shared with him that he needed to get some understanding and awareness as to why his father would physically abuse his mother and why his mother participated in the tragic event over the years. After a few minutes of dialogue, the client came to the realization that his father lacked getting many of his social/emotional needs met as a child and, therefore, he did not have the ability to show love, affection, or connection with anyone. I responded by saying, "Yes, so who is off the hook for blaming and shaming himself?" He gave me a stare and said, "Me?" I said, "That is what I needed to hear."

It is at this juncture that I try to get the client to understand that he is not at fault for behaving the way he did or, in this case, consuming marijuana for approximately twenty years. He did what he needed to do to survive a turbulent environment (smoke weed to not feel and to forget). It was after this clarification that the client had a different outlook on his past and how it affected the way he viewed himself and those he interacted with. He even mentioned that he became a "people pleaser" because he always wanted to be liked, validated, and loved by others because he didn't get those needs met by his father.

Towards the end of our conversation the client's view of his world was a lot clearer. Due to his clarity, the client was given a few projects to complete (at his own pace) while he digested his new information. The client's projects are as follows: 1) He will go back to get his GED since he did not get it when he was young due to him being distracted throughout his adolescent years by his father's life-diminishing behavior. 2) He will learn not to be a "people pleaser." He will think of himself first and take care of his needs first. He will become "selfish." 3) He will recommend to his wife that she doesn't have to scream at him anymore. Her raising her voice at him reminds him of his father's behavior. 4) He will review this conversation with his mother so he can get a better understanding as to why she stayed in such a volatile relationship. 5) He will try to talk to his father about his behavior in the past but he will not have any expectations. He will then come back and we will sit down and review the changes he has made to better his life.

As it was time to go, my client stated he felt a great sense of relief, hopefulness, relaxation, and thankfulness. He said that it was as if a great burden had been lifted off of his shoulders. I explained to him that he'd finally gotten rid of all that emotional baggage he had been carrying around since he was a little boy. Also, he now has understanding and awareness.

CHAPTER 5

"I AM USING A SUBSTANCE; I AM SUFFERING!"

Narcotic abuse and the anatomy of wounding and healing.

"Behavior refers to the actions or reactions of an object or organism, usually in relation to the environment. Behavior can be conscious or subconscious, overt or covert, and voluntary or involuntary." (Source: Wikipedia)

"Human behavior is the population of behaviors exhibited by human beings and influenced by culture, attitudes, emotions, values, ethics, authority, rapport, hypnosis, persuasion, coercion, and /or genetics." (Source: Wikipedia)

Throughout history many people have written about behavior. Here are my two cents as a Deputy Probation Officer. When I was assigned to the Proposition 36 caseload I figured that there had to be a reason why certain individuals used illicit drugs for so long. I continued to wonder why someone would choose to go down that road where the end result was usually a painful, mind numbing experience, which sometimes led to death. This is where an individual had the potential to lose his family, job, self-respect, self-worth, and his life. I often thought, "Don't they see what they are doing to themselves?" Or "Why don't they just stop?" "What are they gaining by participating in this behavior?" These are the questions that would continually run through my mind as I sat down with my clients and how I began the process of understanding the *whys* of their behavior.

Our experiences when we are growing up provide us with imprinting moments that affect us in various ways. It was not until I interviewed thousands of clients that I began to see an underlying pattern of how their behavior was affected by what they experienced from their caretakers during their formative years. I discovered that there was a direct effect on the client's current behavior, which was usually life diminishing, and that their behavior was directly related to what social/emotional needs were met or not met by the caretaker.

How we navigate in the world is directly related to how the world was presented to us as children, which begins in the home. With my clients, I discovered the common denominator was the lack of one caretaker, usually the paternal figure, and at times the maternal figure. It was this upheaval and uncertainty of the family structure that often times propelled the individual to behave in a manner that was more about survival than about connecting with family members or the outside world.

It was during this time in childhood where the majority of the imprinting and mirroring would have the most impact on the client/child. Since our parents are our initial teachers, they are the individuals who have the most impact on how a child views the world.

Now, in most instances, as indicated by my clients, the majority of men (fathers) were not available to have an impact on my clients' childhoods. Most of my clients' fathers were either emotionally/socially unavailable, had disappeared, had run their own business, had served time in state prison or county jail, or they were dead. The male impact or lack thereof, from my experience as a Deputy Probation Officer, has caused the client to interpret their world through "the no father syndrome" filter.

Due to these experiences, my clients created certain judgments about themselves and felt that "he doesn't love me or he would be here with me," "he doesn't care about me because he is gone," therefore, "I must be worthless." These were the images my clients would carry in their memories for years, which would have a direct effect on their behavior.

These are several of the responses that clients would convey to me over the years. I discovered that most of the disruptive behavior is caused by what the parent says or does not say to the child and how the child holds on to and interprets that information in regards to themselves.

Language is one of the most powerful forms of communication we as humans use to interact with one another. Parents are the first individuals whose words can impact the way a child will view themselves and how they will relate to the world around them. It appears the "behavioral pathology" or, to put it in laymen's terms, "life-diminishing behavior" that my clients exhibited in the present or since their childhoods, is directly related to how their caretakers accepted, connected, related, or validated the clients during their formative years.

With a core belief of "I must be worthless" a client is unable to understand why he's unable to make decisions that would benefit his life; because he's essentially wired to self-sabotage anything that would lead to success. This individual is emotionally stuck in the past and is, therefore, unable to make the necessary conscious decisions to transform his circumstances. When a client has experienced years of dysfunction (not getting social/emotional needs met) with caretakers, the client has fewer tools to handle future challenges. One of the ways a client deals with his unmet needs from the caretaker is in using illicit drugs to numb his own emotions and sidestep confronting the reality of where his emotional pain originates. Other ways a client mirrors his childhood experiences is by engaging in violent behavior, criminal activity, and neglecting his own children. He routinely sabotages his own success. He has many short term relationships where he is unable to become vulnerable or intimate with his partner or with any children he has produced. All these behaviors are directly related to how the client perceives himself.

There are certain phrases that frustrate me, especially when I hear them from people who believe a person's behavior is directly proportionate to their age. "Why can't they just get over it?" and "They are adults, they should be able to move on," are just a few of the common statements people announce when they see a person behave in a socially destructive manner. If this were true, we would all be emotionally mature people and would behave accordingly. An individual's social/emotional development can be stifled by an unforeseen traumatic event if it goes unaddressed. An individual can be stuck, emotionally and socially, and never have awareness of how their behavior was impacted by that trauma.

These individuals are hard wired to survive in some way that meets those social/emotional needs. In reality though, they do not know how to identify their needs, are not connected with their needs, do not know how to express their needs, ignore their needs, and are numb to their needs. These are what I refer to as "nice dead people."

This behavior can only be altered if the individual gains awareness and understanding of the behavior. It is at this juncture that the majority of my clients will actually change their behavior—drug/alcohol abuse and dependency—and while they will need support to integrate their new belief system about themselves, they will be self-directed.

How important is the family nucleus in regards to drug abuse/ dependency or any other anti-social behavior? Let's consider the impact of divorce on the child and how that affects their world.

The clients who experienced divorce often told me that they saw the world as an unpredictable, unsafe place to live. When I discussed the beginning of their drug use the clients never thought to look back at the origin of the problem. The clients usually had the tendency to believe their drug use began because they wanted to experiment, they wanted to forget about certain problems, and that their drug use was more of a social matter. I proceeded to ask my clients what they experienced when consuming drugs with a particular group of people. Or "what are you gaining by using drugs with others?"

My clients also had a belief that they were the cause of the divorce. For multiple reasons, children seem to blame themselves for the breakup of the family. The upheaval brought about by the dissolution of the family has to be one of the most devastating events a child can experience. How a child reacts to this traumatic event usually surfaces later on in life, in their adult world. When discussing behavior during adolescence or pre-teen years the clients divulge that they had a lot of freedom and individuality as children/ teenagers and that was when they would join a gang in order to get their needs met for family/community and, most of all, acceptance.

My clients would usually tell me that they hung out with the "wrong" group. I would inform them that they *were* the "right" group; otherwise they would not have associated with them in the first place. I mentioned to the clients that they were getting something out of the deal by associating with certain peers. They were meeting specific social/emotional needs.

Character Pathology Summary

How Through-Line is Created

In my practice of interviewing clients who abused alcohol and drugs for an extended period of time, I go to one place most Deputy Probation Officers don't think to investigate: the place in a client's history when the behavior began. I have always believed that there is a beginning to a behavior.

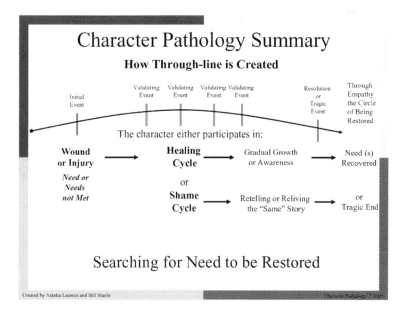

There is a moment where something ignites the process and a chain reaction occurs; it's from that point that the behavior is exasperated. In other words, the behavior becomes part of an individual's "normal" behavior even though the behavior is life-diminishing.

Let's take a look at the graph and I will break it down for you.

Wound or Injury from the Event(s) of the Past:

This is the initial phase where the individual either gets his social/emotional need(s) met or not met by the caretaker during the formative years of his emotional development. If the individual doesn't get his needs met at this stage in his life, then he will begin to see his world as an unsafe, unpredictable place to exist in and develop certain behaviors to cope with his interpretation of the world. After years of life-diminishing behavior the individual begins to adjust to the life around him, learning how to survive by shutting down his emotional development, using aggressive behavior to protect himself emotionally and physically, and using narcotics so he doesn't have to deal with his own reality, to name a few.

Validating the Event (In the Present):

By validating the event the individual behaves in a way that will result in an outcome that he is familiar with. He will continue to repeat the behavior that he believes is the best way to deal with a particularly difficult situation. This is about being the "nice dead person" who does not know how to express or connect to their own needs. This behavior can persist for many years. Drug and Alcohol abuse/dependency is a perfect example of this behavior. The majority of drug use is caused because of an emotional issue. Due to there being many emotions piled on top of many unmet needs, this will cause an individual to become depressed, overwhelmed, or hostile.

Shame Cycle:

This cycle is the cycle that is personally destructive. This is the part of our lives where we continue to relive and retell the "same" story over and over in our minds and there is never a solution. In other words, an individual will continue to make life diminishing decisions believing that his past experiences impact his present behavior.

Tragic End:

This phase has to do with the individual having never gotten their social/emotional needs met or even having an understanding as to why they were never met. Therefore, the individual will always react to the world around him in a life-diminishing way, until he is arrested, incarcerated, or dead. This destructive behavior is attributed to the emotional wounds of the past that they continue to validate.

Healing Cycle:

This is the life-serving cycle. This is where the individual has an awareness as to why his social/emotional needs were met or not met in the past and how he optimistically interprets the world around him because of the needs that were met. The individual, usually for the first time, doesn't blame, shame, or criticize himself or the situation for not meeting his needs. The individual now understands that the past situation or caregivers did not know how to meet their needs. This portion of the cycle actually allows the individual to take the blame off of himself and the caregiver and not personalize it. Now there is gradual growth and actual awareness.

Need(s) Recovered:

This phase is where the individual has an understanding and awareness as to why his needs were never met in the past and is now empathetic to those who were unable to meet them. He can now stop the blame, shame, and self-criticism of himself and navigate the world knowing his caretakers did not have the ability to meet his social/emotional needs. He now has empathy for his caretakers and can put to rest the thought that they intentionally hurt their child. He knows his parents did the best they could with the tools they were given by their caretakers. From this point forward he has the ability to ask for specific social/emotional needs in the moment. He is free from the misgivings of the past and his present state is not affected by the past and his future is filled with unlimited possibilities.

A Client's Story: Wanda

"Wanda" was about fifty years old when I met her in my office for the first time. She stood about five foot four with a slim build and dark skin, and looked as though she had lived a hard life. Her hair, which was unkempt, was wrapped up in a blue scarf to give it some form of order. She was wearing blue jeans that were too big and sneakers that needed to be replaced. Sitting in the chair before me with her arms crossed and legs pinned tightly together, I could tell Wanda didn't want to have to be here with me. I sensed that I represented the authority figure of law enforcement that she had not had positive experiences with. She didn't see before her an advocate for getting free and clean. She stayed reserved and on alert for anything I appeared to be trying to do that she regarded as "psyching her out." For the past fifteen years she had been addicted to cocaine and heroin "because she wanted to at the time." Each time I suggested another reason for her drug use she would simply reply, "No, it was because I wanted to." She wasn't going to budge on her statement. I was the last person she was going to trust.

But then I asked the question of when she started using drugs. She responded in a matter of fact tone. The time she started using heavy drugs was after the death of her father. She clearly didn't want to talk about her old feelings related to losing her father, but I pressed on, gently as I could. I was sensing the presence of an emotional pain associated with her father's death the more we talked about her father, but there would be no moment of understanding or clarity for her or me that day.

Even though she was seeing a therapist, she wasn't ready for me to "fool with her head," so she wasn't sharing anymore than she had to. This was one of those times in my office that I felt frustrated by a client session, and while this had happened before, it was always disappointing. My clients show up to my office because they are ordered to do so by the court. Not showing up would be a violation of probation and could result in an arrest and custody time in County Jail. As their Deputy Probation Officer, I preferred to make a difference, so in this experience with Wanda I grew frustrated, not that I showed it. I was feeling aggravated because I was not able to help her come to understand why she chose to begin to use narcotics and why it was important to her. Wanda was unable to get beyond her state of denial and was unwilling to understand her behavior that day in my office. After our first encounter I never forced her to change her current beliefs. I continued to see Wanda for the next eighteen months and she was reluctant to share with me her reasons for drug abuse and I never pushed the issue. I continued my role as her Deputy Probation Officer, making sure she met the conditions of her probation as that was the most I could do. The way I saw it—as a Deputy Probation Officer who wished to do more—was that I was not able to a make a difference in her life. I was unable to gain her trust, which was necessary for authentic healing to take place.

And in this role that Deputy Probation Officers and Social Workers have, sometimes this is the way it plays out. I had to come to the realization that I couldn't help everyone. I couldn't save all the starfish. So how then does one process this kind of disappointment?

The impulse and drive to help others has always come naturally for me as long as I can remember. I have always found inspiration in watching someone change for the better. As a Deputy Probation Officer with the option to make a difference in a person's life, I had the fortunate opportunity to be involved in a profession to help those individuals in need. During the thousands of interviews over the years, I was fortunate to have impacted the lives of many clients who would listen and apply the information I provided.

However, there were a handful of individuals, such as in the case of Wanda, who for their own reasons decided that the information I had to offer was not something they were willing to embrace. They decided on their own terms that they wanted to continue on a path that they were comfortable and familiar with. Now, for an individual who is impacting many lives for the good, this rejection by these clients was difficult for me to comprehend. If the majority of my caseload was taking the information I was giving them and applying it to their lives, why would these individual's reject something that would benefit them? I found myself imposing my will on these non-conformists. They still wouldn't budge for reasons related to fear of the truth and the pain that reflecting on the past caused.

It took several more rejections for me to come to the point of acceptance that I could not help everyone. Or, not everyone wanted to be helped or listened to or felt inspired to integrate a life changing new idea. I had to finally get my ego out of the way and request their permission to discuss a different way of looking at their drug problem. This different way of relating to my clients has allowed me to learn not to have expectations around what I want/need as opposed to what they want/need from my professional capacity.

What is your role as the counselor or probation officer to the reticent client? Support their journey. Meet them where they are. Challenge them gently when you have an opening but do not push so hard that you shut them down. This is a delicate balance to strive to maintain. The role of a Deputy Probation Officer or a counselor is not to save every starfish on the beach. To save the ones you can who want to be saved is more than good enough.

CHAPTER 6

WHEN BELIEF AND THOUGHT TURNS INTO PATHOLOGY

What are beliefs? Why do we believe what we believe?

Beliefs are the assumptions we make about ourselves, about others in the world, and about how we expect things to be. Beliefs are about how we think things really are, what we think is really true, and what we, therefore, expect as likely consequences of our behavior.

Beliefs are valuable resources, generalizations that people use to give themselves a sense of certainty and a basis for decision-making in an uncertain and ambiguous world.

As a Deputy Probation Officer for clients who have used narcotics for many years since childhood to cope with an unpredictable and dangerous world, I began to understand how they created a certain belief system to compensate for a variety of social/emotional needs that were unable to be met by the caretakers, such as understanding, reassurance, physical safety, acceptance, validation, meaning, and purpose to name a few.

An individual's belief system begins in childhood. What the caretaker believes is directly related to how the child will view his surroundings socially, spiritually, physically, and morally.

If a child had the fortunate opportunity to have caretakers who created a belief system that encouraged self-worth and allowed the individual to express themselves, make mistakes, test personal boundaries, create their own identity, have emotional safety in their presence, and have acceptance, then that child could see the world with endless possibilities. The belief system created in that environment would be as simple as, "I believe I can accomplish anything without fear of failure."

Most of my clients were unable to relate to having a caretaker say words of encouragement about them or words that were supportive. They would always give me a blank look when I asked them, "What would it look like if your parents showed support in whatever you did?" "How would you feel if your father patted you on the back because you accomplished a difficult task?" "How would your world be different if your parents said they were proud of you?" So I shared what my beliefs were, growing up as a child. Basically, I explained to my clients that I was never pressured get straight A's. I was told by my caretakers to do the best that I could in whatever I did. I was never criticized or shamed for making mistakes, so I wasn't afraid to make mistakes or take chances. When I made a mistake, it was only a mistake, and I asked myself, "What did I learn from the mistake and what adjustments do I need to make?" My self-worth and identity were not defined by whether I succeeded or failed, what mattered was that I wasn't afraid to take a chance.

The majority of my clients were socially and emotionally paralyzed by the beliefs they learned as children. Due to their beliefs about themselves these individuals were never able to fulfill their full potential, such as graduating high school, maintaining a job, caring for their child, or caring for themselves. My goal was to awaken them so that they could take care of their own social/emotional needs, so they could self-heal and function in the world without overwhelming doubt and fear.

Narcotic Abuse through Validated Beliefs

Now, as with most of my Probation clients, their initial views of the world usually consisted of uncertainty of home and family and lack of acceptance, validation, and support, to name a few. A belief system that would be created in their world view would be the belief that "my caretakers are unpredictable," "people leave you" (be it death, state prison, abandonment, etc.), or "I have to fend for myself in a cruel and unsafe world that doesn't want me." It is at this point in the client's life that he creates the belief that he is worthless and is unable to move through life in a way that is life serving or with any enlightenment. It is here the client begins to fall under what is called "curses" and "spells." This is where the belief system meets or coincides with the individual's behavior. In other words, the individual begins to display behavior that he believes will benefit him at that time not realizing that the behavior will one day catch up with him, especially when the individual becomes an adult.

In the adult world, the law has a more drastic effect on those eighteen or older, because once an adult gets a case or a felony on his record, that event will have drastic and irreversible effects for the remainder of his life. His decision to continue antisocial behavior will impact how the public views that individual and what organizations are unlikely to hire him with a criminal record. I believe one of the most significant effects comes when the person wants to obtain employment, because employment—especially from a male perspective—signifies whether he can take care of his family, increase his self-worth, and validate his existence. If a man is unable to take care of his family, then he begins to believe that he is unworthy. It is at this juncture where that individual feels rejected and hopeless because he doesn't have any education, specific job skills, social skills, or parenting skills, and will probably be unable to make any advances in his life towards becoming a more productive citizen in society.

Because the client believes the negative image he created about himself to be true, the client begins to behave in a way that will suit his existence. Remember, his behavior is not right or wrong/good or bad, he is getting the majority of his social/emotional needs met the best way he knows how, albeit in a tragic manner. This individual will operate on the premise that "if I am unable to get my needs met at home from the individuals who were supposed to take care of me, then I will get these needs met somewhere else and with individuals who can activate feelings of hope, excitement, and appreciation."

In this case, his needs for acceptance, respect, and security with his secondary family become more important than his nuclear family. For example:

1. If this individual has to skip school to get connection and acceptance with his peers then he will do so, even though it will cost him a high school diploma and future employment opportunities.
2. If he believes it's important to sell drugs to get material things because his caretaker(s) do not have the financial means to support him, then his behavior is justified.
3. If he has to commit armed robbery or car jack an innocent bystander to get respect from his peers, then to him the behavior is worth it. It's the only way he knows how to achieve a particular need.

Distorted as this approach to surviving may be, all is "right" in the world according to him. The behavior we observe from an outsider's perspective causes *us* to point the finger at *his* behavior and judge it as "bad" or "wrong." Unfortunately, society regards this life-diminishing behavior as unlawful.

When Belief and Thoughts Lead to Pathology

Now that I have informed you of how life-diminishing behavior from the caretakers can affect the behavior of their children and how the lack of social/emotional needs has a direct effect on drug use, I want to discuss the "verbal sword." This is where the words of the caretaker leave a lasting and devastating impression on the child. Throughout all my years of interviewing probation clients, verbal scars became one of the most damaging and commonplace scenarios I encountered. The impact of words from the caretaker left emotional scars so deep that those words paralyzed every move the clients made throughout their lives. Clients would inform me of how they never accomplished anything in their lives due to the words that were said by their caretaker(s) many years ago. Or shall I say that they didn't realize it was those life-diminishing words from the caretaker that subconsciously impacted how they navigated their way through life.

When Belief and Thoughts Leads to Pathology

Multiple needs are not met and get manifested into overt or covert life-diminishing behaviors

* **Curses**
  - Wish harm upon; invoke evil upon another person, misfortune, harm or injury to upon a person
  - are taken to or believed to be generated by others (parent/king), the environment or situations instead of constructed by self.

* **Collective Unconsciousness**
  - is a part of the psyche which can be negatively distinguished from a personal unconscious by the fact that it does not, owe its existence to personal experience and consequently is not a personal acquisition.
  - a part of the unconscious mind, shared by a society, a people, or all humankind, that is the product of ancestral experience and contains such concepts as science, religion, and morality.

Beliefs

* **Fixed or Coded Thoughts**
  - "Concepts or Truths" that are amplified and played over and over again creating a conditional and type of certainty and validation that allows an individual to live with in that illusion: minimal, partial or complete.
  - Handed down by society, media, religious, ancestral or institutional: educational, governmental or military
  - These thoughts have at one time been conscious but now have been forgotten or repressed

* **Spells**
  - a verbal formula believed to have magical force a psychological state induced by (or as if induced by) magical words or statements
  - "The needs of the few over the needs of the many"

Corporate Culture Development 2005 ®   Adapted for Character Pathology 2009 ®

Curses and Spells

Some of the most popular spells or curses a caretaker would put on a child that I heard over the years were as follows: 1) "You will never amount to anything." 2) "I wish you weren't even born." 3) "Why are you such a fuck up?" 4) "I can't believe you are so stupid." These statements have caused my clients to become self-critical while consistently sabotaging their careers, their relationships, or any other activity or program they may have tried to accomplish. These are just a few of the comments that stick out in my mind.

I remember when I would have the client reflect on their caretaker's behavior. I would ask them if the caretaker ever made a comment that resonated or had a lasting emotional effect on them during their adolescent years, teenage years, or young adult years? The client would take a moment and reflect. After several moments, a thought would come and they would hesitate and then state that, "My dad told me I ain't worth a shit," or my mother said, 'Why are you fucked up like your daddy?'

I would ask the client, "Do you realize how those comments affected how you see yourself and how your current behavior is directly affected by the comments ingrained in your psyche/mind?" The next question I would ask was, "How did you feel when your parent would make those types of comments?" It was at this time the client would actually, for the first time, realize how he was hurt by those comments. This was the first time many of my clients realized their caretakers were not as caring and supportive as they wanted to remember them. They believed their caretakers were great parents and that they provided for them. So I challenged them further with:

1. If your caretakers were that good then why are you sitting in front of me?
2. If they were great parents then why is your file so thick on Probation?
3. What do you believe caused you to go in and out of jail for the past twenty years?
4. What do you think caused you to abuse and become dependent on illicit drugs or alcohol for so many years?"

These were the questions that allowed them to actually realize how their behavior was directly related to the comments of the caretakers.

Once the truth and the impact of those phrases was understood, often the client would breakdown and cry. For the first time in their life, someone could actually explain their drug and alcohol behavior and how that could be attributed to the verbal abuse by the caretaker in the form of "spells" and "curses."

Past, Present, and Future

This next chart has to do with an individual's past, present, and future. In other words, I discuss with the clients how their past affects their present and how their past impacts their future.

The "events of the past" has to do with the events where social/emotional needs were not met in that individual's past and how the impact of those events continue to affect him in his present day. Based on past traumatic experiences, he will anticipate similar experiences in the future. This thought process causes the individual to continue using his childhood survival tactics.

The "present" is about how the individual views himself today. He is in what is known as his "current condition." This condition is an accumulation of all his events of the past. It depends on how many social/emotional needs were met or not met in the past that will determine how he sees himself in the present.

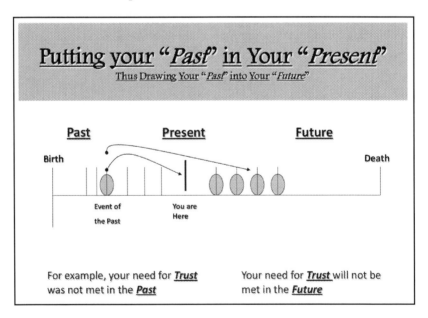

The "future" has to do with how the individual views his future in regards to how the past was presented to him. Because certain social/

emotional needs were not met in the past the individual will believe that those same needs will not be met in the future. The future can be emotionally uncomfortable depending on how he experienced his past. Alternately, with awareness and understanding a person can do something different.

A Client's Story: "I am trapped with no way out."

Today a client came to the office to check in with the kiosk machine. However, he asked to see me because he needed the address to this office. Because of who I am and what I do, I decided to ask him about how he was progressing with his drug treatment. He began to tell me about how he was getting a handle on his disease and was looking for a power greater than himself. It was at this time I decided to pull him into my office and get to the core of his drug use so he could have an answer as to why he began to use cocaine in the first place.

As he sat in my office I asked, "Why do you think you began to use drugs approximately seventeen years ago?" (Note: that he never used drugs before that time.) He mentioned that it was "him"; he had a "sick" mind and the disease was difficult to overcome. Then he mentioned that he wanted acceptance. Now, I can acknowledge that he needed acceptance because he was using with a group of people on the weekends. However, the "I am sick in the mind" is something I have a difficult time accepting, so I continued to probe for the "truth." I asked him what was going on in his life that he had to use narcotics. He mentioned that he had a good job and a good wife, so there was nothing to complain about. So I said, "If your life was so good why would you use illegal drugs?" Then I asked him, "When did you use the drugs?" He stated that it was only on the weekends. I asked him, "What kind of job do you have?" He said that he was a baker for a large food chain. I asked him if he liked the job. He responded that he hated the job with a passion—he worked twelve hours a day in a building where there was no light or any type of movement. The client stated that he didn't want to be there and was feeling frustrated. He did not want to do this job or have this job be his future but he didn't know how to get out it. So, when the weekends arrived, he would meet up with the boys and party hard. When he told me the story, I asked him to think about why the weekend partying with drugs became important to him. After a few moments, he looked at me and said that "my drug use on the weekends was the only time I could express myself and forget about the job I knew I had to go back to on Monday morning." My response was, "Now you have your answer: the reason you used drugs was to meet your need for self-expression, choice, emotional safety, and relaxation (tragically)." He responded by saying that made so much sense. He also stated that the information I presented to him was the truth and that he couldn't deny it. He told me that he appreciated the notion that he didn't have a "sick" mind; he just didn't like his job. To date, the client has a job where he has movement and where he can use his mechanical abilities, which causes him to feel contentment with his life. The client has since stated that drugs are no longer an issue and if he does feel trapped in a given situation he will look for other alternatives that will not get him into trouble.

CHAPTER 7

WHAT THE PROCESS IS
AND HOW IT WORKS!

How is the Needs Based Method® process different?

The process that I use when working with those who have abused or become dependent on alcohol and drugs for a long period of time is predominantly based on Non-Violent Communication (NVC) principles. NVC takes effort to understand and master, but once understood as a communication technique it is a highly effective approach for drawing people out and drawing important distinctions between what is observed, what is felt, what is needed, and how to make requests. NVC assumes that all people share the same basic human needs, and that each of our actions is a strategy to meet one or more of those needs.

With this as the foundation, the Needs Based Method® was developed over time as NVC and other talk therapy approaches were layered and found to work well together. Even before my introduction to NVC and the development of the Needs Based Method®, I instinctively focused on the client's feelings at the time he began using drugs or alcohol. I wanted to know what need was being met by using drugs or alcohol. What was going on prior to this behavior choice?

When supervising probationers or working with clients, my first focus area is uncovering what needs are *not being met* by caretakers and how the lack of those needs influences how the world is perceived and interpreted. Is the world a safe or dangerous place to navigate? The earliest experiences humans have and the messages they receive from their caretakers matter a great deal. With an understanding and awareness of how certain social/ emotional needs were met or not met by caretakers, clients can begin their healing process confident there will be no criticism, blame, or shame for all parties involved; this is "empathy." The individual does not have to live in fear of their past transgressions because they are now "free and at peace" with their past behavior and those who were also involved.

Why it works:

To date, I have used the Needs Based Method® on 8,000 drug and alcohol abusers over seven years. In that time I witnessed my clients making statements such as:

"What did you just do to me?"
"That's so simple."
"I never thought of my drug problem in that way."
"Why aren't they teaching your method in the treatment programs?"
And my personal favorite:
"It makes so much sense."

I know this process works because it became readily apparent that once I uncovered the needs that were being met by using excessive amounts of drugs and alcohol for years, and the feelings behind those needs, my clients reacted with surprise and then relief. I made sure that I never pointed the finger at my clients for behaving the way they did. I gave them empathy and understanding. I discovered my clients appreciated that I did not label them "addicts." They preferred not to be seen as "having a disease." This meant that there was another option to attending meetings for the rest of their lives. Not labeling them gave them hope, self-empowerment, and self-respect. I explained that I saw them as human beings who used illicit drugs and/or alcohol to meet a specific social/emotional need, in a tragic or life-diminishing manner.

The Needs Inventory

The Needs Inventory is a list of needs that human beings require to live on a basic level. When the majority of our social/emotional needs are met by our primary caretakers, we view our life as a wonderful experience. However, if the majority of our needs are not met then the individual will view the world as unsafe, unreliable, and emotionally dangerous. When too many social/emotional needs go unmet at critical times in development, or for long periods of time, an individual will be unable to achieve any self-worth, self-respect, purpose, honesty, and vision in regards to his life.

When I present the NEEDS INVENTORY chart to the client what I am looking for is the client to become clear about what specific social/emotional needs were not being met by their caretaker. The client would review the list and begin the process of choosing which needs weren't met at a particular time in his life. At this time, the client would begin to actually observe, for the first time, what social/emotional needs were not being met and the feelings that were attached to those unmet needs. With choices made on this chart a client can view, for the first time, what his life with his caretaker looks like on paper.

With an understanding as to what needs were not met in the past, an individual can have empathy for himself and begin the process of learning how to get those needs met in the present and in the future.

Basic Needs Inventory

Autonomy: Choice, Self-Empowerment, Independence

Integrity: Authenticity, Core Values, Beliefs, Self-Respect, Purpose

Social/Emotional: (Interdependence): Respect, Connection, Trust, Emotional Safety, Contribution, Stability, Acceptance, Empathy, Validation, Family

Physical Needs: Water, Food, Sex, Air, Shelter

Mental: Understand, Information, Awareness, Thinking

Self-Expression: Meaning, Growth, Skill, Creativity, Healing

Spiritual: Order, Grace, Harmony, Peace, Beauty
Celebration of Living: Movement, Pleasure, Passion, Participate

Adapted from various literature provided by the
Center for Nonviolent Communication

The Four Archetypes (Strategies) of Survival

Child, Victim, Prostitute, Saboteur

One widely accepted view of Developmental Psychology is that our beliefs, characters, and personalities are formed during childhood through a combination of nature and nurture. Indeed, during the first two decades of life we make our first promises to ourselves to provide for and protect ourselves, assuming we can. Many people have said that as adolescents they promised themselves they would never be physically abused or humiliated again, but it is harder to follow through on this promise when we feel powerless.

During early childhood it is important to understand that our sense of personal power depends on the quality of our physical lives (food, water, shelter) and on our ability to survive with the help of our caretakers. As we get older we begin to interact in the physical world and begin to distinguish between right and wrong as situations present themselves. From these interactions we develop our self-worth and self-esteem, if this development is impeded the ability to make favorable choices will be diminished or prevented.

These four primary archetypes—the Child, Victim, Prostitute, and Saboteur—represent our greatest life challenges and how we choose to survive. Together they represent our various personal issues, worries, and vulnerabilities that cause us to negotiate away/compromise our power within the physical world.

What I believe to be important about these archetypes is that they influence how we relate to our power because of material wealth, how we act in response to authority, and how we make choices. These archetypes are in essence neutral, even though their labels are charged with negative implications. They have two channels for expression: light and dark.

These four archetypes are the close companions of your gut instincts, or in other words, intuition. They can provoke you or make you aware of how helpless and weak you feel in your situation and your fear of being victimized. These archetypes can expose how you sabotage favorable opportunities. However, in the future these archetypes can become your allies in fulfilling goals and dreams.

According to Carolyn Myss in *Sacred Contracts*, "The more conscious you are about the patterns that influence your behavior, the more likely it is that your choices—and the lessons you get from them—will be positive." (pp. 112 Sacred Contracts, Myss)

The Child: The Guardian of Innocence

Out of all archetypes that I have witnessed and experienced in my clients over the years, the Child archetype is what I consider the most common. Why? Because as children these are the archetypes that will establish our perception of our world due to how life is presented to us. The majority of my clients fall into alignment with what I would refer to as the "Wounded Child," the "Abandoned Child," or the "Orphan Child" because many of my clients did not get the majority of their social/emotional needs met. After thousands of interviews I can say with conviction that 98% of my clients were raised in dysfunctional families where there was a lot of pain, suffering, neglect, and uncertainty. When these traumatic events occur at various stages of development this causes the individual to become emotionally/socially stuck at that stage.

Therefore, the "child within" creates specific methods in order to survive in his environment. This "child within" is familiar with neglect and abuse and believes that is how his world functions. As we get older our bodies grow chronologically, but unfortunately the "child within"

(Wounded, Orphaned, Abandoned) does not change. This archetype becomes stronger, ready to anticipate the expected fear, pain, and neglect that was experienced as a child.

The challenge for most of my clients is to have the social/emotional maturity that should have developed as they became adults. Unfortunately, if these stages of development were not fulfilled or completed in childhood, then my clients would discover that it is difficult, if not impossible, for them to be independent and responsible for themselves in the adult world and establish healthy relationships. Hence the inability to complete school, connect with their own children, stop illicit drug use, or establish healthy relationships.

This process of development is how human beings would ideally like to mature. Unfortunately, if the inner Abandoned, Wounded, or Orphan Child did not receive the nurturing that was necessary during their formative years, those aforementioned archetypes will reveal themselves in other areas of their life. What happens next is that the individual will spend the early years of adulthood trying to understand, heal, and make up for those deficiencies.

The Victim: Guardian of Self-esteem
The Victim archetype is another prevalent behavior that manifests itself in the majority of my clients because it is based on common fear. Many of my client's become a Victim when they are unable to get social/emotional needs met. They have also suppressed many of their negative emotions (anger, confusion, helplessness, rage, guilt, shame) because they were victimized by someone who was bigger and had more physical power than them. They experienced varying degrees of child abuse and neglect by a caretaker. I had clients who decided to use the Victim mentality to gain sympathy and continued the strategy by not standing up for themselves because the behavior met specific social/emotional needs. Understand too, these clients do not know of any other way to function in their world. As a

Victim they have no power nor do they have independence. It needs to be understood that the core issue for the Victim is whether or not it's worth giving away their own sense of empowerment so as to avoid taking any responsibility for their independence.

The key work for the Victim archetype is to examine their relationship to power and their need to construct personal boundaries, especially in interactions with those individuals with whom there are control issues.

To heal, the Victim archetype must create new belief systems around self-esteem and personal power. The problem or threat that the Victim is trying to overcome and the power/ammunition that is needed to do so must be named for the transformation to become tangible and fully integrated. When feeling threatened or suspecting a lack of the appropriate social, professional, or personal power, a person in Victim mode must take notice of their state physically, emotionally, and mentally in order to "unplug" and be able to restore a sense of personal power again.

The Prostitute: Guardian of Faith

The majority of Prostitutes I have met in my years as a Deputy Probation Officer have been drug/alcohol dependent. Their inability to make different choices and get out of their life-debilitating environment is directly related to their issues of self-worth. I have observed the Prostitute archetype as one of the most prevalent survival mechanisms my clients have used to remain alive if their world is one of chaos, instability, isolation, and self-worthlessness. The Prostitute archetype can manifest itself in subtle ways and in normal, day-to-day circumstances. When an individual's survival is threatened, the Prostitute archetype shows up. The most important question a person accessing the Prostitute archetype can ask is: How much of themselves are they willing to give up or sell? Will they sell their integrity, their intellect, their word, their body, their morals, or their soul—for the sake of meeting the physical need for survival and security?

For example, many of my clients told me that they were unhappy and miserable; they were constantly getting arrested, going in and out of jail, unable to get a job, using illicit drugs, having no place to call home, never feeling accepted, and feeling there was no one to talk to. Yet, they continued to engage in a behavior that diminished their self-worth and took away their freedom because that was the only way they knew how to live. The dynamic of the Prostitute archetype is to test the power of the person's faith because a person with faith cannot be bought. And without faith, a person will not have the strength to turn down the asking price.

Chances are every time a step toward personal empowerment is taken there will be a test that challenges the Prostitute archetype. Someone will want to buy a piece of his soul to render him less powerful and make them more powerful.

This archetype can be transformed into a guardian but it requires confronting the Prostitute within.

Prostitute energy appears when an individual stays in a relationship that is not good for him because he sees staying as better than being alone. This archetypal energy also appears when he's asked to do something unethical or illegal "for the good of the company."

It may be hard for an individual to accept, but the people who trigger the Prostitute in him represent his most painful relationships. Prostitute interactions allow or force us to confront our fears of survival, and for this reason they are often terrifying and humiliating.

The Prostitute archetype can also act as a guardian that alerts the individual to situations in which he must decide to "take up his bed and walk." Once he steps away from a circumstance that is costing him too much—money, energy, dignity, or time—lasting transformation becomes possible.

The Saboteur: Guardian of Choice

I have spoken with many clients over the years and discovered that the majority of my clients have this common belief about themselves, which is a fear to take responsibility for themselves and for what they create. I have noticed how life-diminishing comments and experiences from caretakers have caused many of my clients to deliberately destroy or cripple any attempt to be socially, emotionally, or financially successful.

I have listened to many of my clients inform me that they have created a nice life, which includes having a job, family, and a home. Then, after a period of time, they will get uncomfortable with their success and will eventually sabotage it by using drugs, getting arrested, having affairs, or getting fired from their job.

They need to understand that the saboteur within them may be the one most closely linked to their ability to survive in the physical world. It is often their fear of being without the basic needs in life—such as food, security of home and family, acceptance, and emotional safety—and their social and personal contacts that allows this archetype the power to torment the individual.

I have seen that the only way to decrease the power of the Saboteur is to be courageous by acknowledging the patterns of thought and behavior that arise when it shows up; the individual should trust his instincts and make the decisions that will require life-enhancing change in his life.

Initiation (Rites of Passage)

A ritual or ceremony signifying an event in a person's life is indicative of a transition from one stage to another as from adolescence to adulthood.

Ceremonies can mark important transitional periods in a person's life, such as birth, puberty, graduation, having children, marriage, and death. A Rite of Passage usually involves a prescribed procedure of activities and teachings with the purpose of stripping individuals of their original roles and constructing new roles for them.

For example, "the traditional American wedding ceremony is considered a rite of passage. In many earlier societies, some of the most complex rites of passage occur at puberty, when boys and girls are initiated into the world of adults. In some ceremonies, the initiates are removed from their village and may undergo physical mutilation before returning as adults." (Cultural Dictionary)

Rites of Passage are the fabric from which most cultures around the world are made.. It is with this sense of routine and established cultural behavior that gives the culture a sense of purpose. For example the Jewish culture has a Bar or Bat Mitzvah for their young people when they come of age. This is where the child becomes aware of their physical changes (puberty) and begins to take responsibility for their own actions.

In the American South, the term "debutante" is used to introduce a young woman to society when she reaches the age of maturity and is eligible to be courted. The significance of this practice is to introduce her to eligible bachelors and their families within a select group, based on social status.

Another form of initiation is that of the first haircut. In the United States the first haircut is considered a landmark event for the child and is marked by saving a lock of hair. This practice of the first haircut occurs on or around the first birthday and usually happens in a barbershop. This is especially significant for black children as the barbershop has been the social core in the African American community.

The rite of passage that is celebrated in the Latino community is called a Quinceañera. In this ceremony the girl/woman carries a doll that is dressed like her, which is intended to represent her childhood. After the girl dances together with her father, he will exchange her flat shoes for heels. Once the shoe exchange has taken place, the father, symbolically, has the Quinceañera girl/women abandon her childhood and accept her new role as a woman

In the United States, the "sweet sixteen" birthday social gathering is celebrated to symbolize the coming of age of a young girl from childhood to adulthood.

I wanted to learn about several examples of diverse rituals that cultures use to signify the stages of development for their children. It is important to understand the impact that ritual and/or tradition has on a child's sense of purpose and belonging. Therefore, I wanted to see for myself what the impact was on individuals who did not have a sense of who they were, where they came from, or where they were going in regards to family traditions. In this next section I will discuss the impact of the lack of tradition and ritual with my Probation clients.

According to Robert Bly, one of the most disturbing protests that entered American society is what I call the "Man Child Syndrome." The maturation from child to adolescent to teenager to young adult to adult has been crippled by our "consumer society," which mocks all initiation and ritual as a meaningless and primitive form of community interconnection. The product of this cultural dismissal is the creation of mothers who are disappointed in their sons because they continue to remain dependent on them for many years. On the other hand, women have added difficulties because they are disappointed when they run into the problem of finding a man who is independent and able to take on the responsibilities of fatherhood.

"What could a 'second birth' mean to our culture? The initiation traditions ask that the young initiate 'die,' and then receive a second birth, which is often symbolized by receiving a new name. For us, it means in part that the young man or woman is offered a way out of the meaningless consumer society. If the consumer society is determined to hold to literalness, if it continues to mock all initiation of boys and girls, slandering all ritual work as primitive, then we will have disappointed mothers whose sons remain dependent on them at forty years old; young women who have disappointments of their own, and who are also disappointed when they can't find a man adult enough to take on the responsibilities of fatherhood; AND disappointed young men, who cannot struggle with their father in the real world or the symbolic world. Such a son endures an unfruitful suffering, which consists in never being able to move away from his mother's doorway. Such young men will waste much of their life before they receive the 'new head' that gives them power over worlds." (pp. 81 *The Sibling Society*, Robert Bly)

"The father's absence is so pervasive in the sibling society that the mothers now carry an enormous burden; and mothers, no matter which community they live in, know how immense the burdens are that they carry alone. We know that the rituals we have, pitiful and unimaginative, are not working, because the boys are killing each other despite the mother's care." (pp. 86 *The Sibling Society*, Robert Bly)

When I read this passage it reminded me of how our culture as a whole does not practice a rite of passage experience with our young people. The words had such an impact on me that I now know how important a social transition period is for the human experience, especially beginning from adolescence to young adulthood.

In the past eight years I have interviewed over 8,000 clients, the majority of whom were men on Probation. Over the years I noticed a pattern of behavior and I began to speculate as to what was the common denominator between each of my clients. I wanted to know if they had any transitional phases in their lives. In other words, what I wanted to know was: Did they experience any social/emotional changes from early adolescence to teenager to young adult? From the stories that were shared, it appeared the majority of my clients experienced some form of trauma at an early age and because of this experience they were unable to make the transition from one social/emotional developmental stage to the next. It was as if those past experiences were directly related to my client's becoming emotionally "frozen" in time.

As a Deputy Probation Officer, I would regard most of my clients as "men children" or "women children." This wasn't about labeling them; it served to create an image of what was occurring inside them. What I mean by this statement is that these clients live and breathe in their adult bodies; however, they are functioning, emotionally, in their childlike state between the ages of six and twelve depending on when the trauma occurred. It was as if they were stuck in that moment of time, when the tragic event occurred and they were never able to detach from that experience, which is directly related to their behavior in the adult world.

I began to see, hear, and understand that the majority of my clients were frozen in time in response to the tragic events they experienced and were basically trying to survive in their current world condition with the tools they were given by their environment. The majority of the clients I interviewed informed me that there was rarely anyone home to guide and teach them about what was expected morally, socially, or educationally when they reached a certain age/stage in their lives. My client's would spend years without parental supervision or nurturing between having an absent father and a mother who worked long hours to attempt to provide for them.

When interviewing these clients, I discovered that the majority never had that series of transitional ceremonies that would identify each stage of social accomplishment. There was never a celebratory period of moving from being a toddler to an adolescent to a teenager to a young adult to an adult.

Between 85% to 95% of my clients came from single-parent households, where the father was absent and the mother was in a near constant state of being overwhelmed as a single parent. When I asked about their extensive drug or alcohol use, the majority of my clients began their drug use on or about twelve years of age. There were instances of the client consuming drugs and alcohol from the age of six or seven. There were times when the client would emphasize that he believed it was normal to use drugs as an adolescent because he saw his caretakers or relatives consuming drugs/alcohol. There were times when their relatives would leave half-filled cups of alcohol lying around the house after a party or times when drugs were offered to the client as a child.

Those clients who began to use drugs at ten to thirteen years of age indicated that this was the time in their life where they realized that many of their social/emotional needs were never going to be met by the caretaker. They believed it was in their best interest to leave the home and get their social/emotional needs met by those whom they believed would meet them, such as their neighborhood gang, friends, and other family members. They resorted to using drugs/alcohol to meet their need for being accepted by others and also to numb the emotional pain they experienced from the neglect of their caretaker.

Underage drinking and drug use is a behavior that has become a devastating form of initiation but an initiation none the less. The big difference is that these clients are creating their own rites of passage. The belief, in their mind, is they are trying to move to the next level of social development by creating their own rules about what they believe is beneficial for their meaning, purpose, and existence. Unfortunately, without the necessary information and support from their caretaker, the choice to drink and use drugs so early in life usually has a painful conclusion.

Another opening question I ask my clients is if they had the opportunity to graduate from high school. If a client completed high school that bit of information informs me that there was some degree of constant support from the caretaker who believed it was important to complete this part of pre-adult life. Unfortunately, the most common response I heard was "no" because there wasn't a caretaker, especially a primary male figure, to stress the importance of getting a basic education or to guide them into the next stages adulthood. If the response was "no" I would ask them: "Wasn't there someone in your life who would emphasize that having a good education would give you better opportunities in the future?" I would literally get this puzzled look of confusion. It was as if I was asking them to perform some impossible task, like cutting off the cable TV and enrolling in school. To them, having a man of significance like a father, mentor, or coach to guide them from childhood to adulthood is a foreign concept. The idea of someone showing genuine interest in their social/emotional development was never an option and, therefore, they could never know the importance or impact of that experience.

So, I decided to take it upon myself to be, what I call, their "Probation Father." I wanted to see if I took a vested interest in their lives, would they be able to take in the experience of someone informing them about what could be done if they were given the information that could enhance and change their lives for the better. I decided to begin the project by informing those clients who did not have a high school diploma or G.E.D. (General Education Degree) that it was time to go back to school and complete that project. I noticed by asking that initial question the clients gave me a look, again, of surprise and disbelief. My clients were surprised that someone had faith in them and believed that they could actually accomplish this task. Again, I must reiterate that they never had anyone actually challenge them to do anything. For most of my clients, I was the first person to take an interest in their education or to even offer the idea that they could actually pull this off.

Having this experience with my clients led me to the question that if 90% of my clients were not going through a rite of passage, then what is the rest of the U.S. doing with their young people? I can only imagine how a young person in this day and age will find it impossible to understand the importance of experiencing each stage of his life and how those stages can help turn a lost child into a well-functioning adult.

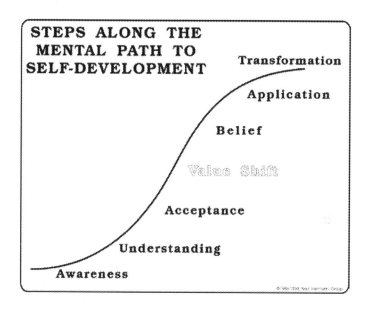

Herrmann posited that there are effectively seven steps along the Mental Path to Self-Development:

Awareness: Having knowledge or perception of a situation or fact. Conscious.

Understanding: To know thoroughly: to grasp or perceive clearly the intended meaning or cause.

Acceptance: Agree to receive or do something that is offered or proposed; take on responsibility or liability.

Value Shift: Social principles, goals, or standards held or accepted by an individual, class, or society, etc. (shift to move or change from one position to another)

Belief: An acceptance that something exists or is true, especially without proof; a family-held opinion or conviction.

Application: The act of putting something into operation: put into practical use or relevance.

Transformation: To change the conclusion, nature, or function of; to convert; to make it suitable for a new purpose.

In order make any changes in life, a person needs two of the basic steps in the beginning of the process to achieve those goals. Awareness and Understanding are the initial steps I focus on with my clients because it is at this juncture that the client will get his needs for information, clarity, and understanding met with regards to where certain emotions, behaviors, and thought processes originate.

After these two steps are realized and the client's initial questions are answered, he now can move to the third step: Acceptance. I inform the client that this is the step where he needs to give himself permission to not continue to punish himself for what he did in the past (behavior) but accept that he was meeting his social/emotional needs with the information that was given to him by his caretakers. In other words, "You did the best you could under the circumstances you were given." Basically, he learned to navigate and survive in an environment where certain behaviors were accepted, such as gang activity, drug use, criminal activity, neglecting their own children, and dropping out of high school. Now once I get them to accept their past behaviors they can unload all the blame, shame, guilt, judgment, and criticism from their conscious and proceed onto the next phase of development.

The fourth phase of the program is the Value Shift. This is the phase where they can begin to make different choices and decisions that are life serving as opposed the decisions they made prior to them not having any understanding or awareness of their behavior. It is at this phase I can actually witness a client's dramatic change in his decision making process, self beliefs, and how he views the world. He understands that many of his social/emotional needs were unable to be met by his caretaker and how that impacted his behavior and beliefs over the years. At this stage the client becomes more empowered in his decision making process and now has empathy for those individuals (family, relatives, friends, significant partners) who impacted his past life (childhood) in a tragic manner. It is here that he can actually breathe a sigh of relief and begin moving in a way or direction that is more emotionally free flowing and natural.

The fifth phase, or Belief phase, is where the client changes his old belief system to a new belief system. He now understands how his old beliefs were formed by what he observed in the past and/or what he was taught by his caretakers, usually during childhood. Due to his awareness and understanding of the past he now believes in what he has learned and applies this new information in the present day. However, now that he has decided to accept, learn, and apply his new beliefs into his life, he must be aware that those individuals who knew him before the Value Shift may not be as accepting of him; he now represents what they are needing and does not behave in the same manner as he once did.

This brings us to the sixth phase of Herrmann's Mental Path to Self-Development, which is Application. This is the phase where the client begins to apply all the information that he learned in the previous five phases. This is the area where he begins to change his behavior by interacting differently with those individuals who impacted his life, usually the caretakers. The individual now knows what social/emotional needs were not met, how that affected him, and now will ask to get those needs met. On the other hand, if those needs are unable to be met, he now knows not to take that experience personally and, more importantly, he knows he is not at fault or to blame for the other person's (caretaker's) inability meet certain needs. He is now healing his past and does not shame or guilt himself for the behavior of his past. He fully understands that he was only doing what he knew how to do at that particular time in his life.

The Transformation phase is the final stage where the individual applies all of the information at a subconscious level. He now moves through time and space with ease and confidence without thinking about old beliefs and behaviors. He just does it. The individual has actually transformed himself into a human *be*ing as opposed to a human doer. Because of his changes he will now have an awareness and understanding of the world around him, the ability to identify what he is feeling and needing at the present time, and the ability to make decisions that will benefit himself.

A Client's Story: "We almost lost our daughter…"

It was another busy day at the office. I must have seen about 3 or 4 clients by 11am. Some clients require more effort than others that always made my job more interesting. Day to day in my role, I didn't know what crises I would encounter. Nonetheless, I am always up for the opportunity to impact someone's life positively. Over the loud speaker, I heard my name being called to pick up an emergency call on line 1. So, I took a deep breath getting myself prepared for anything.

I picked up the phone, pushed the transfer key, and said, "Mr. Oden speaking. How can I help you?"

A man launched into talking with panic in his voice, "My daughter is on a meth binge and is running the streets. I am scared that she will hurt herself. She is 19 years old and has been using drugs for the past 5 to 6 years. We keep trying to help her but for some reason she does not respond. This episode seems worse. I don't know what to do or where to turn. I called your office to see if you have any suggestions about where to send my daughter." He repeated with anguish in his voice, "I just do not know what to do."

As I listened, the Rolodex of past client stories in my mind began to churn. I had heard some version of this scenario so many times in the past decade, and I did know how to help. I told the man on the phone to bring his daughter to my office as soon as possible even though this young woman was not presently my client. Helping her and her family was what mattered to me at that moment.

He asked me about the idea of having his daughter enter a treatment program.

"Have you ever enrolled her into a treatment program?" I asked knowing full well the answer.

"Yes," he replied.

"How did that experience work out for you?" I asked calmly.

"She has run away from every treatment program she has ever entered," he replied with frustration.

"If you want to find out "why" your daughter continues to use then I recommend you bring your daughter to my office today so we can talk and get some answers. I have interviewed thousands of drug/alcohol dependent individuals, and I can help your family, but I need you all here together for starters."

The father responded, "I will be there in 30 minutes with my daughter and her mother."

"Ask for me at the front desk," I said. I then hung up the phone and cleared a two hour window to be available when they arrived.

30 minutes later, I picked them up in the front lobby. I walked them back to my office and positioned the chairs so I could have the daughter seated directly in front of me and the parents to my left. Sitting before me was a Caucasian family. The mother was in her late 30's with shoulder length brown hair and a medium build. She was casually dressed in white capris pants and a flowered rose colored top. The father was casually dressed in jeans, a grey short sleeve sweatshirt and sneakers. Both parents looked scared, tired, and anxious.

I had placed the daughter strategically in front of me. I wanted to be able to focus on her and had symbolically separated her from her parents. She looked like she had been through a meat grinder. She was skinny with blotchy skin and brown stringy hair. The dark circles under her eyes were a dead giveaway; she was an avid meth user. She appeared to be strung out. I knew I needed first to gain her trust in order for her to relax and be forthcoming with her story. So, I looked right into her eyes. I let her know that she was in good hands. Together we were going to uncover what was causing her so much emotional pain. She nodded her head in agreement and said, "Thank you."

I then turned to the parents and asked them to tell me their story. I wanted them to tell me any childhood experiences their daughter had that might cause her to react in this life-diminishing manner. The mother spoke first. The man sitting next to her was not her daughter's biological father. They had been a couple for several years. She added that she and her boyfriend were ex-felons, and each had been involved in the criminal justice system for many years.

As a young woman, the mother had herself engaged in using drugs. She had been abandoned and neglected by her father. Her own mother had tried to be there for her, but was emotionally frail as her own mom had not been consistent. Years later as a young mother herself with no paternal support she had used drugs and would leave her daughter by herself for days at a time in order to satisfy her drug fix. The mother shared that she had left her daughter with strangers over the years. I watched the tears well up in her eyes and stream down her face as she told her stories and looked over at her daughter.

The daughter said nothing while the mother spoke about her own past. The mother looked down at the floor as she realized for the first time how her behavior had impacted her daughter. She insisted emphatically that all that was behind her. The mother and her current companion were doing well in life, working a business together, making enough money to pay the bills, and staying out of trouble.

I asked the mother if she has changed her life for the better? I asked her, "What makes you so sure that you won't go back to your old ways of behaving that involved drugs use and leave your daughter behind? She insisted that she has learned her lesson and did not want to live in desperation anymore. I asked her, "Does your daughter know that?" She gave me an inquisitive look. She said, "What do you mean?" I said, "Just because you trust the fact that you have changed, your daughter might not yet be convinced."

I turned to the daughter and asked her to look at the "needs" sheet and pick out your most important "need." She scanned the sheet and chose the word "trust." I asked her why she had picked the word "trust."
"I believe my mother will leave me again like she did when I was a child. I don't believe she will keep her word, so I am waiting for her leave me again," the young woman said flatly.

I looked at the mother and saw that she was crying. I grabbed as many tissues as I could offer her to soak up the tears. For the first time, the mother understood her daughter's pain. She admitted that she did not realize how her behavior impacted her daughter's mistrust of her mother's new behavior of staying put and staying clean.

I looked at the mother and suggested she tell her daughter how much she had changed. "Tell her how you will care for her this moment and in the future." The mother took a deep breath and began to speak. "I am a different person than I was many years ago. I was wounded and neglected. I did not understand how I was hurting you."

The mother got up and leaned in and looked her daughter in the eye. She told her clearly and gently, "I will never leave you again, and I will always be there for you.

I watched as an invisible wave of relief washed over the daughter. It was as if she was longing to hear those words, from her mother, many years ago. The daughter began to cry as a sign that she accepted her mother's edict as true. The mother let out a sigh of relief and held on to her husband who had just watched this whole emotional and social transformation unfold right in front of him. The husband could hardly believe, with his own eyes, what he just witnessed.

I sat back in my chair thankful. I knew that each person before me now had more clarity and understanding about the past events and the behaviors surrounding the most recent events. The past had been haunting the daughter, and she didn't trust that her mother would stay put. That her mother would leave was always in the back of her mind. Even though the mother had created a positive change in her own life, the daughter did not know if the change would be constant or not. Therefore, she acted out with her methamphetamine dependency. The daughter's behavior was one way to have her mother constantly involved in her life tragic as that reasoning was.

I asked the family to come back a week later, and they all agreed. What a difference a week makes. This family had come into my office full of panic and uncertainty.

A week later I greeted them at the door, and I noticed smiles and joy on their faces. The mother told me that she couldn't believe the transformation and the difference that one visit made. I looked at the daughter and noticed she gained some weight and appeared very receptive and just plain happy. The mother and father thanked me from the bottom of their hearts and were grateful for what I had done for them. I felt a sense of relief and joy knowing that I had made a difference in their lives. I watched them, at ease with each other and smiles on their faces, walk out of the building one last time. I will never forget that newly found smile as the daughter held her mother's hand knowing the world for her could be a much safer place.

CHAPTER 8

THE CONCLUSION: THE FINAL STEP

Confucius : The journey of one thousand miles begins with a single step.
You've arrived at the end of this book (almost). I hope that you have come to understand some key points that I believe to be critical to healing and recovery from drug/alcohol dependency. It's been a journey of discovery for me in regards to understanding the "through-line" of the ongoing epidemic of drug dependency and how it impacts families, communities, and society at large. It's an ongoing journey. For as much as I have learned, I know there is always going to be more to understand in this work I continue to do with energy, compassion, and commitment. As stated in the introduction, to date I have interviewed over 8,000 clients who range from being self-made millionaires with advanced degrees to welfare recipients without a high school diploma and a criminal record that stretches back for decades. At one time or another all these individuals consumed illicit drugs for many years of their lives and were arrested for doing so. They each succumbed to drug/alcohol abuse and dependency even though these individuals came from different social and economic backgrounds.

Social and economic privilege did not protect a person from getting hooked on illicit drugs. It did not matter how much education a person had or how financially secure a family was. If the rich and the poor, the educated and the uneducated could fall into this drug trap then there had to be something that all these individuals had in common. Some didn't use drugs till later in life in response to a tragic life event such as a divorce, loss of a job, death of a loved one, or something else that triggered an overwhelming sensation of helplessness. Yet, every last client had a basic set of social/emotional needs that were never met and therefore they used drugs/alcohol to fulfill the emotional chasm of those unmet needs.

If someone is propelled to use drugs in response to traumatic conditions, maybe starting drugs and using drugs was the easy part. As the counselor I am, I know that coming to understand the truth behind drug use can be the most difficult and painful aspect of recovery. This is why understanding a person's journey is important to me. I believe that once a person understands their past experiences and how those experiences <u>have</u> influenced their behavior, they now have the conscious ability to shift their behavior and belief system.

One of my favorite authors is Joseph Campbell, who uses storytelling and cultural communication to describe the human experience. The central pattern most studied by Campbell is often referred to as the "Hero's Journey." The "Hero's Journey" describes the typical adventure of a selected individual known as The Hero (you). The Hero is the person who goes out into the world to learn about himself and what he must do to achieve great deeds on behalf of the group, tribe, or civilization he is part of. After the journey, he returns to the group to inform them what he has learned about himself.

Stages of the Hero's Journey

There are twelve steps to the hero's journey. According to the <u>Oracle Education Foundation Library</u>, those steps are as follows:

1. **Ordinary World**: This step refers to the hero's normal life at the start of the story, before the adventure begins.
2. **Call to Adventure**: The hero is faced with something that makes him begin his adventure. This might be a problem or a challenge he needs to overcome.
3. **Refusal of the Call**: The hero attempts to refuse the adventure because he is afraid.
4. **Meeting with the Mentor**: The hero encounters someone who can give him advice and ready him for the journey ahead.

5. **Crossing the First Threshold**: The hero leaves his ordinary world for the first time and crosses the threshold into adventure.

6. **Tests, Allies, Enemies**: The hero learns the rules of his new world. During this time, he endures tests of strength of will, meets friends, and comes face to face with foes.

7. **Approach**: Setbacks occur, sometimes causing the hero to try a new approach or adopt new ideas.

8. **Ordeal:** The hero experiences a major hurdle or obstacle, such as a life-or-death crisis.

9. **Reward**: After surviving death, the hero earns his reward or accomplishes his goal.

10. **The Road Back:** The hero begins his journey back to his ordinary life.

11. **Resurrection Hero**: The hero faces a final test where everything is at stake and he must use everything he has learned.

12. **Return with Elixir**: The hero brings his knowledge or the "elixir" back to the ordinary world, where he applies it to help all who remain there.

In regards to drug/alcohol dependency, I do not like to tell probationers that they are addicts or they are sick. Rather, I take them on the "Hero's Journey" because it allows them to see where they are with their drug use at the moment and what efforts it will take in order for them to get to the "Supreme Ordeal" (that ultimate fear) and, finally, have the "Elixir" in hand (self-realization). This storytelling form allows the individual to see the social/emotional journey they will need to take in order to gain an understanding about their drug/alcohol dependence and what they can do to change their behavior.

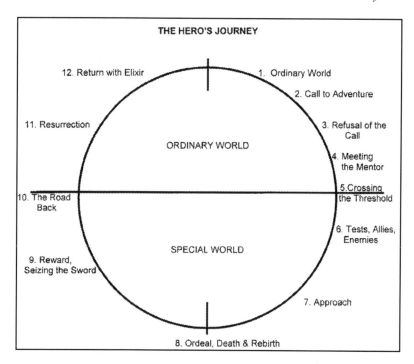

THE HERO'S JOURNEY

12. Return with Elixir

11. Resurrection

ORDINARY WORLD

10. The Road Back

9. Reward, Seizing the Sword

SPECIAL WORLD

8. Ordeal, Death & Rebirth

1. Ordinary World

2. Call to Adventure

3. Refusal of the Call

4. Meeting the Mentor

5. Crossing the Threshold

6. Tests, Allies, Enemies

7. Approach

The twelve stages of the Hero's Journey as experienced by those who are afflicted by drug/alcohol dependence translates in this way:

1. The Ordinary World: This world is where the drug/alcohol dependent individual functions in everyday life. The individual is using drugs/alcohol excessively, making decisions that they believe are beneficial. At this time in their life, drug/alcohol dependency is normal and it is what helps the individual deal with their painful reality. First, understanding what their Ordinary World is allows me to identify with that individual and empathize with their dilemma.

2. The Call to Adventure: The individual is thrust into action, now the adventure can begin. In this case, the drug-dependent individual now realizes that his drug/alcohol problem poses a threat to himself, his family, and to his community. The individual realizes he must take action and take on the challenge to do something about his drug/alcohol dependency so his life is not destroyed.

3. The Refusal of the Call: At this stage the individual may want to accept the challenge (to get off drugs/alcohol), but unfortunately personal doubts and fears may cause the individual to fail to take the necessary step to change. The individual knows that consistent drug/alcohol use is not good for him; however, he is comfortable in his state of suffering, denial, and lack of awareness. The familiarity of his current condition is a lot more comfortable than the road to recovery and the unknown.

4. The Meeting of the Mentor: The purpose of the Mentor is to dispel any doubts and fears the individual might incur and give him the competency, courage, and resourcefulness to begin the next stage of the journey. *This critical meeting assures that the individual will come to see the importance of his personal challenge.* During this stage, the Mentor (counselor, friend, teacher, and/or therapist) will give insight, guidance, or provide essential lessons on self-worth regarding the drug/alcohol problem so the individual can refrain from using illicit drugs/alcohol.

5. The Crossing of the Threshold: At this moment the individual has decided to commit himself to the journey and once done realizes there is no turning back. In this case it is getting off drugs/alcohol. Whether he is willing (by choice) or unwillingly (by an arrest, DUI, or divorce) shoved into change, either way he makes the decision to move from the world that he knows (current drug/alcohol use) to the world he does not (Judicial System, Probation, AA/NA meetings). He has decided to do something about this problem even though it is the first time he will actually look at the genesis of his drug/alcohol issue.

6. Tests, Allies, Enemies: Now that the individual is out of his comfort zone, he must anticipate a series of challenges that are more difficult and will test him in a multitude of ways. Now that he has decided to do something about his drug/alcohol issues, he must be aware of those obstacles that are thrown in his path of personal growth. The individual must be aware that there will be people (enemies) who are willing to

sabotage his progress and must learn to overcome these challenges in order to reach his ultimate goal of sobriety. The individual will need to discover whom he can and cannot trust. Along the way, the individual will learn who will become his allies and who will become his enemies. It is at this stage where his newly discovered powers and skills will be put to the test, and he will gain a deeper understanding of his character.

7. The Approach to the Innermost Cave: At this stage the individual begins to look within himself to understand the inner conflict that he has not had to face until this juncture. The individual will need to look at his fears and uncertainties that surface as he takes this journey. In other words, the individual will gather information about his past traumatic experiences and make sense of how these experiences relate to his excessive drug/alcohol dependency. The individual, at this stage, must take in what he has learned about himself and be prepared to face those traumatic moments or persons/caretakers that cause anxiety, fear, and pain throughout his life. Once the individual is ready to face his fears (family trauma that is directly related to his drug/alcohol dependency) then he is ready for the Supreme Ordeal.

8. The Supreme Ordeal: This portion of the journey represents his "innermost crises" or "traumatic experiences" that he will need to face and conquer in order to survive and for his world to change for the better. In other words, the individual will need to empower himself to face those past experiences that caused him to depend on illicit drugs/alcohol and no longer allow those learned beliefs and negative feelings to be numbed by drug/alcohol dependency. This is the defining moment for the individual because everything he has learned and now understands is put on the line. If the individual fails to come to terms with the cause of his trauma then the individual will continue to suffer (relapse). In other words, the individual's fear of facing his demons will continue to haunt him and another relapse will

likely occur. However, should he face the demons, what awaits him is the Reward (emotional freedom).

9. The Reward: In this stage the individual has confronted and defeated (the Supreme Ordeal) his greatest fears (verbal abuse, neglect, physical abuse, drugs). The Reward can come in many forms such as, greater insight, forgiveness of others, greater knowledge, and empowerment. At this moment the individual (the Hero) has the right to celebrate. Once the individual has finally conquered his greatest personal challenge he is transformed into a new condition of awareness and understanding about his drug/alcohol dependency. The individual will be able to use this new information to create a better world by becoming emotionally free and at peace with himself, effectively overcoming his greatest fears, having slain his personal dragons (past traumatic experiences).

10. The Road Back: In this stage the individual must make an internal decision to recommit himself to going back to the Ordinary World. He can prepare to go "home" with the information (the Reward) that he has learned about himself. The individual now has self-approval and absolution, emotional freedom, or even personal forgiveness for his past drug-dependent behavior. The individual understands that he doesn't have to carry the emotional burdens he has believed since the traumatic events took place. However, he must be aware that there are individuals he will confront who do not accept his change and will do anything in their power to pull him back into their world of drug dependency. At this moment he chooses his own personal objective, which is to remain drug free.

11. The Resurrection: It is during this stage of the journey the individual (the Hero) is "reborn" or transformed through his experiences, the lessons he has learned, and the people he has met along this journey. The individual (the Hero) must now prove that he has achieved new insight and understanding and willingly accepts his new Value Shift/ Beliefs as being beneficial to his life. Due to the information he has

learned from his mentors the individual who was drug dependent now understands that he was never the cause of his drug dependency. He is free from self-blame, shame, and guilt because of his new understanding. Thus, the individual is "reborn" because he now knows the truth of his situation. In other words, he understands that his own caretakers may not have gotten their social/emotional needs met as children, which affected how they raised their own. Now he can empathize with his caretakers, whether they are alive or not. He will now apply his lessons learned to his new life.

12. The Return with The Elixir: This is the final stage where the Elixir brings closure to the journey and the individual (the Hero) returns to his home and his new way of life. The individual has matured as a person, learned through experience, faced his fears, and has won. He now looks forward to applying his new state of awareness in starting a new life. The individual now looks to his allies for support and will shun his enemies. The drug-dependent individual now clearly understands his new outlook on his life, himself, and where he has been. He will share what he has learned about this journey with others. The individual will return to his home where it all began but he now knows that things will never be the same again.

In my roles as counselor and Deputy Probation Officer, taking my clients on their own Hero's Journey, I have witnessed repeatedly what happens when an individual understands their pain and knows where their problem originated. It is a liberating moment. Then of their own volition, they can shed their negative beliefs about themselves and change their behavior (e.g. drug/alcohol use) to effectively alter the course of their life.

It is my hope that those who read this book and those who work with clients with a substance abuse issue gain an in-depth understanding of their client's journey and what prompts their drug-dependent behavior. My focus is always to discover and uncover how the emotional component they have experienced over the years impacted their choice to become dependent on drugs/alcohol. Even those who believed they had a great childhood upon closer examination begin to see cracks in the veneer of their story.

I do not impose my will on these individuals by instructing them to stop using illicit drugs/alcohol. My focus is to wake them up and to get these individuals to understand why they ventured in the direction of drug use in the first place. To me, their understanding of their home-life experience spoke volumes because they did not connect their drug use to their caretaker's inability to meet many of their social/emotional needs during the formative years of development. Once this understanding is identified, the emotional burden that has been carried through the years can be released. And asking powerful questions is how I started a chain reaction. Examples of powerful questions I often asked are:

1. How old were you when you started using drugs?
2. What were the events that occurred during your initial use of drugs?
3. Tell me about your relationship with your father and mother?
4. Tell me what your caretakers said to you or did to you that is frightening or painful to remember.
5. How did using drugs make you feel? Or, what did using drugs do for you?

Some Final Thoughts

The many clients I have worked with in the past ten-plus years remain a source of inspiration each time I begin work with a new client. I strive to help every client come to understand why they started using drugs/alcohol in the first place, regardless of whether or not they choose to stop using. In more than 80% of my clients' experiences, a natural by-product of understanding why they started is the catalyst; first they choose a shift in values and beliefs and then they can choose a change in behaviors. And, because it is their choice, it is more likely to be a lifelong change. Now, they can also understand their parents better (empathy), accept that they were not the "bad kid" (self-empathy), and accept responsibility for their actions and choices during that time.

And, that makes all the difference in how they choose to live their life moving forward.

The United States makes up approximately 5% of the world population and consumes a disproportionate amount of the world's illegal drugs. As a witness, I see drug abuse as prevalent as ever. We are far from winning the war on drugs. Alcohol and drug abuse has increased to epidemic proportions in America and continues to overwhelm our society and will continue to have a detrimental impact on all of us if all we do is maintain the status quo.

What I have observed over the past thirteen years, regardless of socioeconomic background, is that people do not really understand how personal events impact and trigger their feelings, thoughts, beliefs, and behaviors. It is unfortunate to say that most people do not have full awareness or understanding as to how their collective environmental and personal experiences impact their interpretation of themselves and their place or role in the world.

What I am basically always attempting to do is wake these people up at a social/emotional level so they can realize how the impact of the neglectful or absent caretaker affected their social/emotional development.

WHAT I am effectively saying to every client I work with in the approach I take, the questions I ask, and how I treat them during my time with them is:

1) To understand the impact of their family dynamics.
2) To understand their caretakers and what they experienced.
3) How to have empathy for themselves and their caretakers.
4) How to stop the self-blame and self-shame cycle.

"Please stop blaming yourself for your drug use, rather take full responsibility for your past choices and learn how to accept that those who raised you did the best they could based on their own upbringing. Understanding this generational cycle that you have been subjected to opens up the possibility for you to feel empathy for them as well as empathy for yourself."

It is at this "Aha" point that true, deep healing and recovery becomes possible and the likelihood of relapse diminishes. I wish I could say that I have been successful with every person who has crossed the threshold of my office door. I am like the man walking down the beach with an endless number of starfish before him; I will assist the ones I can, one by one.

Experience informs me that alcohol and drug abuse is not a disease. Some people do choose drugs and/or alcohol as a coping mechanism for surviving traumatic experiences; unresolved traumatic experiences can drive an individual to begin consuming drugs/alcohol at a destructive level so the traumatic event can be dealt with or tolerated. And, I have worked with and interviewed so many clients whose common denominator was the impact of the absent, abusive, and/or neglectful father or caretaker (which, by definition, is a traumatic experience).

These "adult children" are often repeating the same pattern of abuse with their own children. These individuals will likely cheat on their spouses, abuse drugs, neglect their children, and eventually break up the family. I wanted something different for them in their futures.

I can't say enough how critical it is that a child's social and emotional needs be met during their early years by their caregivers. I know my professional colleagues understand this too. What then can we do to heal the Wounded, Abandoned, or Orphaned Child that lives on in a person who is chronologically an adult?

Fifteen years (and counting) I am committed to doing what I can in my role as a Deputy Probation Officer and counselor, and as a mentor and educator. I clearly see how my own childhood experiences prepared me well for the work I do with enthusiasm, compassion, and a sense of urgency. As shared in the introduction, I believe things happen for a reason and there is synergy at work in my professional history. I also know there are a lot of people in the helping professions—be they Therapists, Counselors, Social Workers, or Deputy Probation Officers like myself—who feel like I do. We spend our hours working with deeply troubled clients and wanting to support their full recovery from addictive behaviors and long-term substance dependency. I know it is what I want for each and every client I have ever had interactions with—whether it comes to be a reality or not. I have a genuine desire and intention to facilitate deep healing and long-term recovery that improves the quality of life of the individual and their family and communities.

This "documentary-style" book is my best effort to contribute working solutions, practical tools, and techniques for counselors to employ and for clients to follow. For Deputy Probation Officers, Counselors, and Social Workers in particular, using the strategies and methods in this book can assure that more Probation clients complete their Probation requirements and leave the criminal justice system behind for good.

My hope is that I have created a resource that can and will be enthusiastically used by people in the helping professions—Counselors, Social Workers, Deputy Probation Officers, and Educators—and that more people in recovery from addiction get both clean and free and stay that way!

> *My clients tell me, "I am clean!"*
> *I reply, "I hear you tell me you are clean. But are you Free?"*
> *This is the question that starts their journey.*

APPENDIX A

Excerpts of Real Life Cases from a Daily Diary

Day to Day: Real Life Cases from Proposition 36 clients

About California Proposition 36

Proposition 36 was designed to provide support for offenders of non-violent drug related crimes. The intent of the program was to provide substance abuse treatment instead of jail time. Clearly, Prop 36 was a controversial piece of legislation and it yielded results that are deemed both positive and negative. I was curious enough to go behind the scenes of drug dependency to find out more about what caused my clients to think, feel, and behave the way that they did. I am grateful for the opportunity to learn and understand my clients' journeys of personal suffering and be a catalyst for their healing.

The University of California, Los Angeles made the required evaluation of Proposition 36 and has issued three annual reports on the implementation and impact of the program since 2003. These reports provided data and analysis that helped state legislators determine the future of the program from year to year. A UCLA study released in April 2006 showed Proposition 36 to be saving taxpayers $2.50 for every $1 invested. According to the Drug Policy Alliance, total savings for taxpayers over a period of five years totaled $1.4 billion. Another UCLA study found that convicted drug users had become more likely to be arrested on new drug charges since the proposition took effect.

I am personally glad for the opportunity I had to work with over 6,500 clients because of this program. From the beginning of my work with Prop 36 clients, I made it my practice to keep notes for the sake of being the most effective I could be from visit to visit. I wanted to be able to chart their progress, remember their breakthroughs, and keeping notes allowed me a means to do so. I offer a sampling of client notes I kept as an Appendix to illustrate what I did and what was working.

It is my hope/aspiration that reading these excerpts that I kept in their original form sheds light on how much each individual changed over the course of months or even years because of the conversations we had about their illicit drug use and its origins.

Even though these dialogues were conducted over a decade ago, I can honestly say that nothing has changed with the war on drugs except for the fact that illicit drug use has gotten worse. The National Institute on Drug Abuse indicates that illicit drug use has increased 8.3 percent in the US since 2002.

What that latest statistic tells me is that how we socialize and nurture our children continues to be a deciding factor in how they navigate through life as adults. As long as there are single families, absent fathers, emotional abuse, neglect, and continued family dysfunction there will always be illicit drug use.

These chosen selections represent a real-time month and are actual excerpts from the notes I kept during the years I worked specifically with Prop 36 clients. In order to meet the need for privacy and respect of the clients the names have been changed. These excerpts have been edited for the purpose of presentation in this book, but the content has remained intact.

November 13, 2006

Victor, Hispanic, thirty-nine years of age, reported to the office today. He has been reporting since July of 2006. In reviewing Victor's former problem, it is safe to say that he has now, for the first time, established a relationship with his mother. He mentioned that he didn't have a relationship with his mother when we first met; hence his drug problem. I have been working with Victor for the past four months to get him to understand his drug problem so he can stop using and also rebuild a relationship with his mother. Victor was abandoned by his father, and his mother had to work multiple jobs to keep food on the table and a roof over their heads. Victor stated the treatment counselor is giving him a difficult time because he is doing well and doesn't have the urge to use drugs. Victor keeps informing the counselor that he is doing just fine; however, the counselor doesn't want to hear it. Victor finds the whole thing quite funny. Victor continues to inform me that he is finally "free."

*****

Diego, a twenty-seven-year-old Hispanic male arrived today for his mandatory monthly report-in obligations. Diego has participated in a residential treatment program for about a year. He is now out of the program, working, and doing quite well with his life. Diego's drug problem was the result of not having any father figure and his mother worked constantly. At the time of his drug use, Diego believed that no one cared about him because no caretaker was ever home to give him the necessary attention that he needed to become an emotionally healthy adult. About three months ago we uncovered all the social/emotional needs that were never met by his father and mother as a child and since then Diego has looked at himself and his life differently. He has come a long way. Diego continues to move through life with much more ease, confidence, and self-worth due to his understanding as to *why* he used drugs, which was to meet his need for emotional safety and acceptance from others. He has reestablished a relationship with his mother and has empathy for what his father did not have the ability to do or not do, when it came to being a father.

To date, Diego is not attending AA/NA meetings and the treatment counselors are having a difficult time understanding why. Diego explained to the counselors that he is at peace with his past and therefore he doesn't need to hide anymore. Diego stated that the counselors continue to question his ability to stay clean when not attending meetings. Diego says he gets frustrated because there is nothing he can do to convince the treatment staff that he is doing well and that he doesn't need to attend the meetings.

Diego also stated that he believes the treatment facilities do not work and knows he was fortunate to have met me, a person who was willing to search for the truth about his drug use. He stated that my technique made so much sense that he wished my method could be taught throughout all the treatment facilities.

I asked Diego if he would write a paper about what he experienced in the treatment facilities. He said he would be honored.

*****

Kenny, a forty-one-year-old black male, came for his initial visit. Kenny stated that he did not use drugs; he was caught with twenty grams of crack inside a ring box he'd picked up for a friend. The friend was dealing drugs and Kenny wasn't aware of that. Kenny is now stuck in a situation he does not know anything about, which is drug/alcohol dependency. So now I have an individual who doesn't use illicit drugs but has been ordered to attend an out-patient treatment program. Kenny will have to sit and listen to stories that involve alcohol and drug abuse over and over for the next six to nine months. I decided to give Kenny an overview of what I do so that he would have some understanding as to how and why people use drugs for extended periods of time. He stated that he was really amazed at the information I was giving him. He agreed to give his point of view as to what he observed throughout his treatment obligations while on Probation.

November 14, 2006

Sam came by for his initial visit. Sam is an elderly/middle-aged black man who is suffering from kidney failure. He is currently on dialysis. I don't think there will be any testing. Sam's health problems are due to a long life of drug use and not drinking water.

Sam came down from Utah. He and his mother were introduced to my teaching methods about a year ago. She continues to support her son because of his health issues. Since our time together, Sam claims their lives have changed for the better, especially his mother who was involved in an abusive relationship with her husband. She continues to use the techniques I taught her and Sam on her stubborn husband and claims has gotten her self-respect back. When she and Sam come to the office she always mentions how grateful she is and cannot thank me enough for helping her reclaim her life.

November 15, 2006

Today was cloudy and relatively cool. It was as if I was in London. The day started off calm due to mild client activity. I decided it was a good time to catch up on files that seemed to be lingering around for no apparent reason. The reasons, I believe, could have been many; such as a continued court date, client in custody, or the file just plain disappeared. I always say, "One must always go through the heap of files to see what can be sent to someone else's desk, hopefully never to return." I sent away some files for my clients who had completed their Probation under the umbrella of Proposition 36. It always puts a smile on my face to know these clients listened and applied the methods I taught regarding their drug issues and how their lives are now better for it.

*****

Paul came in today. He called a few days ago stating he would enter into a treatment program because he wanted to detoxify. Paul is a white male, over fifty years old, who comes from a family of fifteen. He has been drinking and using cocaine since the age of thirteen. I have been working with Paul for over a year but he doesn't want to hear what I have to offer and he also doesn't want to report once a month as instructed. These are the clients that are considered trouble. Nevertheless, I decided that since he'd spent the last fifteen days in a treatment facility I would try to introduce him to my methods and see if I could get my point across.

Paul stated that he felt fantastic for the first time in years now that all the alcohol was out of his system. He mentioned that he loved the program and would return for another fourteen weeks. So, I said to Paul that "I appreciate that you are feeling much better and that you feel confident being in the treatment center. However, how are you going to handle yourself when the treatment ends?" and "Did you actually learn *why* you consumed alcohol and drugs for the past forty years?" He gave the same old response, "I don't know." My goal at this time was to get him to understand that he had been hiding or running from *something* for over forty years and when he decides to look and see what that "something"(event(s)) is he will begin the healing process and drug dependency will no longer be an issue. He gave me that canned response that he has a disease. I almost lost it. I said, "You have got to be kidding me! You aren't falling for that '*story*,' are you?" Since I don't raise my voice too often he was kind of frightened. I explained to him that I didn't want him to become dependent on meetings for the rest of his life. However, I did mention it would be beneficial to attend meetings out of fellowship, not out of guilt or peer pressure.

So, with my voice still raised, I asked the big question: "When did you begin to use drugs?" He said at thirteen years of age. I asked, "Why so young?" He said he was working. "Why were you working at thirteen?" He said, "My father wanted me to work." His father said it would make him a man. So I asked him, "How did you relate to your father?" He said,

"He was excellent, a very good man." This is the part where the fantasy of the parent overtakes the reality of how the situation really was. I repeated, "How did you relate to your father and him to you on a social/emotional level?" After several seconds of thinking about it I prodded him by asking, "Did he yell at you? Did he hit you? Did he hold you? Did he hug you?" He said, like they all say, "He was a good man." "I am not asking if he was a good man. I am asking how he behaved toward you." He finally admitted that his father was very strict due to having fifteen kids. He said, "My father made my sibling work at young ages because if they wanted the good stuff they would need to buy it themselves, if they didn't want work they would get the Sears brand." I asked him to give me an example as to how his father treated him. Paul stated that one time his father shaved his head because he came home late one night. So I asked him, "Did your father ever tell you he loved you?" He said no. "Did he ever show physical affection toward you?" I pointed to my family pictures on the wall, the one with me holding my son. He said no. "Do you have any idea what hugging/holding is about?" He said no. He stated that he had a very strict upbringing and did not get a lot of attention or affection due to the amount of children they had. I said, "We are finally getting somewhere." I mentioned that once he understands certain childhood events and he works to heal those childhood wounds he will be an emotionally free man. He stated he would be willing to listen. I told him that I appreciated him for listening to me and I wished him Happy Holidays and that I would see him in mid-December.

November 16, 2006

A first-time client reported to the office for his initial orientation regarding his Proposition 36 obligations. The gentleman, Vincent, a forty-three-year-old black man, is married with two girls and one boy. He is currently residing in a residential treatment facility and has been for about one year now due to his continued relapses.

As I usually do, I asked the question, "Why do you think drugs became an important part of your life?" And he stated, "It is not important." I informed him that everything we do is important, otherwise we would not waste our time doing whatever it is we do." He gave me a puzzled look. Nonetheless, I decided to get right down to the core of the problem because I always believe it is important for my clients to gain understanding and awareness as to why they do what they do, in this case, using cocaine for over twenty years and relapsing every three to six months.

I asked him to describe his childhood to me and how he related to both parents. His initial response was that he had a really good upbringing and that he was allowed to have anything he wanted. As I kept probing he continued to inform me that he was an only child and that his father had never been in the picture. He was raised by his mother.

As I probed deeper into his life I asked the questions that I believed would eventually lead to the answer as to why drugs continued to play an important role in his life. The client mentioned that his mother did almost everything for him as a youth. He mentioned, once he thought about it, that she never let him make any decisions on his own. She was always in his life no matter what he did, even as a teenager.

He decided to leave the house at eighteen years of age and join the military. It was here that he believed he would gain his identity and independence. I asked him what were the similarities between how he was treated by his mother and how the military treated him. He gave me a puzzled look and didn't quite know how to answer the question. After a few minutes, I gave him a hint. I stated that "your mother and the military were the two institutions that were constantly telling you what to do." After he left the military, the client stated that his mother was back in his life telling him what to do again. I asked him, "How do you feel when your mother continues to make your decisions?" He stated that he gets angry, frustrated, embarrassed, and helpless because he is always made to be helpless.

Once we uncovered his mother's constant intrusion into his life the client gave me that look of surprise and astonishment because, now, his whole life with his mother seemed to make sense to him. For the first time in his life someone had made sense of his past, his decisions, his relationship with his mother, and the influence she had on him.

Now the next part of our discussion is to understand where the drug use came into play. This is the tricky part. As I began to probe the area of his drug use, the client mentioned that he would use drugs whenever his mother would make an important decision for him. The client again gave me a look of wonderment. He couldn't believe what he was hearing. So I put two and two together for him. I informed him that when he utilized drugs he was getting his need for autonomy and choice met.

In other words, "That is a moment in your life that you get to make your own decision to use without her permission. Also, the drug use numbs your feelings so you do not have to experience the anger, frustration, and helplessness you have toward your mother because you rarely had your needs for choice and independence met.

"Now, on a deeper level, the other reason that you continue to choose to use drugs is that getting caught casts you in the 'little dependent boy' role. Your mother needs you to play this part in order for her to continue to have purpose and meaning in her life. In other words, if you were to grow up to be a man and were able to make your own decisions, your mother would not have any meaning or purpose in her own life. So, the more mistakes you made in your life the more your mother would come running to save you and nurture you back to health, but only for a short while. She may have been secretly or subconsciously hoping you would fall down again so she could help you get back up and continue the cycle. If truth be told, she kept you as the 'dependent' little boy so her life had purpose."

The client couldn't believe what he was hearing. It was as if he had a ten-ton rock taken off of his back. I told him I wasn't finished yet. I needed more information for myself and for him to understand. So I asked him, "Is your wife similar to your mother? In other words, is she constantly telling you what to do?" He gave me a blank stare and an embarrassed "yes." I needed him to understand that what we learn in childhood and how the world is presented to us as children is, usually, what creates the behavior we will take with us into adulthood because the experience is familiar to us. So, I said in plain English, "because your mother was your only parental role model and she never gave you choice or independence, it reinforced your belief that women are the decision makers; therefore, you subconsciously chose a woman who possessed the same behavioral characteristics as your mother."

After that quick assessment, the client slumped in his chair and gave me a dazed look. He stated he could not believe what had happened to him. He could not believe what he was hearing. He stated that the information was too much for him to grasp. I agreed and mentioned to him that getting to the root of a drug problem can be overwhelming. However, before we conclude our first session I always want my clients to state what need they were meeting by using illicit drugs. The phrase used by all treatment facilities is "Hi, my name is Vincent and I am an addict." After our sessions, my client's days of using this phrase are over. My client's new phrase will now look and sound like this: "Hi, my name is Vincent and I used drugs for many years to meet my needs for choice and independence in a tragic manner because I was feeling angry, frustrated, and hostile due to my mother's need for purpose, meaning, and validation."

I left him with one final thought to consider before he returns to the office next month. I told him that he needs to assert his "man" within and that we will learn how to shrink his "little boy" so he can be the man of the house. His first assignment before he came back to me in December of 2006 was to cut the turkey for Thanksgiving.

November 22, 2006

Another client came to my office and, again, I gave him the same verbal assessment about his drug use, how it started, when it started, etc.

Joseph was a black man, over forty, who had used narcotics since he was a teenager. He's been married a couple of times and has a few kids, his latest addition is a four-month-old baby girl.

Joseph stated he started to use drugs when he was about twelve or thirteen years of age. I asked him to explain to me his family dynamics. He stated that he was the second youngest of five siblings. He had a sister eight years younger. He didn't know his father and had two older brothers who ended up in prison by the time he was a teenager. His two older sisters and his younger sister and mother were his family.

What I am trying to do is paint a picture so I can see how my client, Joseph, navigated through his life. Over the months of probing Joseph's past I begin to piece together a sort of timeline of events, how he interpreted those events and how those events affected his behavior throughout his life.

What I saw was one man surrounded by four women as all three other lead males were no longer part of the family dynamics. That scenario prompted me to ask questions. For instance, "What do you thinks goes through a mother's mind when she loses three of her lead males and there is only one left in the family?" He gave me a puzzled look. I said, "Now think about it, you are the only male left in the family." Then he gave me a surprised look and stated to me that he was spoiled. I said, "Now we are getting somewhere. Remember, you are their prized possession and they are only doing what certain women do, mothering the boy." He couldn't believe it and stated that it made total sense. He stated that since he was about ten years old and the older brothers went to prison, the family let him get his way with almost anything.

So I inserted the drug use question. When and why did drugs become so important in his life? The client mentioned, now that I brought it to his attention, that he began to use drugs when he got into an argument or when he didn't get what he wanted. I said, "BINGO." He stated, "That's it?! When I don't get my way in life I get very angry, throw a tantrum, and I use drugs to show them that they can't tell me what to do?"

Once he heard the nature his drug problem the client was overwhelmed with joy and relief because he finally had an answer as to why he'd behaved in such a way for such a long period of time. I explained to him that as a child he was given too much autonomy, choice, and freedom. I explained to him that he took that belief of entitlement and brought it to his adult life and continued to behave in the same manner.

Now, his drug problem is stated as such: "Hi, my name is (blank) and I used drugs for many years to tragically meet my need for choice, being heard, and autonomy." I also mentioned to my client that his new saying doesn't absolve him of his responsibility of drug use; however, it does clear up what needs were being met by understanding what he does.

Joseph now has a new outlook on his life and now knows he can overcome his drug problem by getting a better understanding and awareness as to when and why the years of drug consumption were important. Too much autonomy given by the women in his family unintentionally caused the client to believe he was entitled to have or do anything he desired.

Joseph's next visit will include a review of our initial meeting and how this awareness has affected his outlook on his life.

November 29, 2006

A Proposition 36 client came into the office today for orientation. His profile is as follows: Daniel is a thirty-seven-year-old black man, single, living with his mother. Daniel was arrested for sales and placed on Proposition 36.

Daniel was raised by his mother. From the age zero to fourteen Daniel had your typical single-parent upbringing. His situation allowed him freedom, choice, and independence. He stated his mother had him participate in football, basketball, and baseball all through high school due to the fact that he was hyper. During the first fourteen years, Daniel stated that he had a lot of freedom and independence while growing up. At the age of fourteen, Daniel asked his mother about his father. Daniel's mother replied, "You don't need him." It was after that remark Daniel became angry, hostile, and frustrated. He said he stole a car and sold it to a chop shop. He began ditching school. Daniel stated his mother was working all the time and he still didn't have anyone watching over him. He stated he began drinking in his junior year of high school and continued until his sophomore year of college.

Daniel did receive a football scholarship to San Diego State in 1988. However, Daniel believed school to be one big party and didn't attend classes so he was dropped from the program after his sophomore year.

At the age of twenty, Daniel worked for UPS for three years and was fired for calling out sick too often. During his twenties he moved to Las Vegas and did house jobs or floated around from job to job. He soon moved back into his mother's house.

At the age of thirty-two, his mother had had enough of his behavior and finally said, "NO." This reaction shocked Daniel who was used to getting his way with his mother. So, Daniel sold drugs for a few years and made a lot of money. He sold for about three years before he was arrested and put on Proposition 36.

After reviewing the life of Daniel and I began our discussion about how boys are affected by not having a father in their life. I was curious about the fact that his mother made such a harsh comment about his father when he asked about him and wondered how that comment affected him. Daniel proceeded to tell me that he was a product of date rape and that his mother moved from central California to Los Angeles so that she would not be subjected to the ridicule of family, neighbors, and friends.

Now that I knew the core of his anger and displacement I had a place from which to work and expose all the needs that were never met by his mother and his father. I explained to Daniel that his mother gave him too

111

much autonomy as a child and that he took full advantage of the situation. I explained to him that his mother's absence wasn't intentional but was due to his mother needing to work. Also, the area that jammed him up emotionally was the lack of a male role model. "There was no one to guide you, give you boundaries, or show you the male perspective of the world. So, our objective is to find your 'man' and shrink the influence of your 'little boy.'" I explained to him that his little boy was created and never allowed to develop because he was never held accountable for his actions and he always got his way as a boy. When he didn't get his way Daniel would resort to drugs or the behavior of a child throwing a tantrum. Daniel became a drug dealer to meet various needs. His initial need was financial. Then I explained to Daniel that he also met his need for acceptance, respect, being liked, validation, community, self-respect, and self-worth. Daniel gave me a look of shock, stating that I made total sense. I explained to him that all the social/emotional needs he didn't get from his father or mother are what he received from his clients by selling drugs. The last question I asked before he left my office was, "What do you want to be when you grow up?" He did not know how to answer the question. I said, "What do you want to do with your life?" He responded by saying no one had ever asked him that question. I explained to him that if I was his father these are the types of questions I would ask. So, I concluded our conversation by telling him to think about our conversation and get back to me next month. Remember, men take care of business; boys run, hide, and play.

****

My next client, Freeman, is a twenty-four-year-old black male with a high school diploma who was arrested twice for DUIs. He'd spent a year in a residential treatment facility not really learning why he drank so heavily on those two infamous days. He had already been in my office a couple of times but, as I always do, I wanted to review our last discussion so we could continue forward.

This conversation became interesting because I didn't really know why alcohol became a problem until I asked him what his reasons were for using excessive alcohol. When he told me it was because of a break up with a girl I began to see who my client was for first time. I said to him, "You're really sensitive aren't you?" He said, "No!" I said, "Yes, you are. You are the kind of person that cares a lot about other people." He gave me a questioning look. I asked him, "Did you break up with your girlfriend or did she dump you?" He said, "She dumped me." I asked him, "Why do you think that happened?" He didn't know. So I asked him about his life as a child.

Freeman stated his bio-dad left him when he was one and a half years old. His mother remarried and Freeman never warmed up to his stepfather even though he tried to bond with Freeman, he rejected any or all emotional needs his stepfather attempted to meet because he was not his real father. Freeman also mentioned the rivalry between his stepfather and himself over his mother. He didn't like the fact that his mother had another man in her life.

What really hurt Freeman was the fact that his bio-dad was in and out of his life, but mostly out. The events that really hurt Freeman were when his father promised to pick him up to spend time with him and he never showed. Freeman remembers waiting for his father for several hours. This happened many times. It was these events that would lead Freeman not to trust anyone who came into his life.

So, what Freeman and I uncovered was that he began to cling to his girlfriend because he was so happy to have someone to love him. She became overwhelmed and could not handle his emotional needs and decided to leave. I told him, "These problems arose because of your father's inconsistent behavior regarding connection, acceptance, reliability, and lack of emotional safety." When Freeman listened to my explanation he stated that it made total sense. He stated he was somewhat relieved to have an answer as to why she left him. I also explained that "your father's behavior probably made you not trust anyone who came into your life." He said, "That's correct." I said, "So now I hope you can see why you drank so much on those two days when you were arrested. To me, it appears that those were two days where you were emotionally overwhelmed and needed to numb your pain of rejection.

"Now it's time to get you back on track with your life. From this point on you and I will take a journey that will show you how to heal and become the man your father never allowed or taught you to become. This may not be easy but it will be worth it. Are you willing to take this journey with me?" He responded with a resounding "yes."

December 5, 2006

Today Arlis came by to get some much needed perspective. Arlis was my client about four years ago. He returned to me because he relapsed on cocaine again. My client was ignored by his grandmother and abandoned by his father when he was younger. My client's grandmother would separate him from the other kids because he had darker skin than the others and was embarrassed to admit my client was her grandchild. (Arlis is of Spanish descent.) I remember discussing his story with him some four years ago and he broke down and cried. I also remember discussing the absence of his father who had, I believe, several families going on at one time. This discovery was a hurtful awakening for my client. My client was rejected by his grandmother and his father and, therefore, used success and accumulation of material things to validate his self-worth.

My client graduated from college, had a six figure income, a huge house, cars, etc. The one thing he didn't have was validation and recognition from those who were most important to him, his father and grandmother. My client would need constant validation no matter where he traveled, how much money he made, or what he possessed, so he became a people pleaser.

Now on this day, my client explained that he relapsed because his sister was very angry with him for taking his brother-in-law out on the town and letting him end up having sex with another woman. The brother-in-law stated to my client he has not had sex with his wife in the last three years. Nonetheless, my client was more upset over his sister being angry with him. What happened was that those old feelings of his family abandoning him had resurfaced and were too great to overcome, so he went to his emotional safe zone: cocaine. My client cannot stand anyone being angry with him or disliking him, especially his family, and he will do anything to avoid that situation.

Today, my client decided to give me his reasons for being in this predicament. He proceeded to tell me that once he had a drink that he had an "allergic" reaction. I almost fell out of the chair laughing so hard. I said, "You have got to be kidding me!" He kept emphasizing that old way of thinking. I continued to suggest that he'd better not forget about how his grandmother ignored him and his father abandoned him as a little boy and how he carried that belief of "I am worthless" into his adult belief system and behavior. I informed him that "your beliefs lead you to please everyone you meet or you become afraid to connect with someone because they might leave you." I had to get him to listen and understand his behavior over the years about the social/emotional needs that were never met by his grandmother and father. I needed him to have empathy for his grandmother and father as to how they saw the world and how their view of the world and themselves affected their relationship with him as a child and as an adult.

My purpose is to get him to understand why he relapses when his "little wounded and abandoned boy" is threatened by a family member or significant other. In other words, he believes he has disappointed his grandmother, the experience of which still lingers within his mind and is transferred through his family, which he thinks has disappointed.

After about twenty minutes of explaining the needs and feelings and how they were interconnected and how those needs that are not met will tragically be met in some other way. At the end of our session, my client finally had a better understanding of his behavior and how his past continues to manifest itself. I gave him the packet and information about the "truth about treatment centers." He stated that he would read it. However, he still has reservations about letting go of the old methods of the twelve steps and AA/NA meetings. I let him know that "if attending meetings meets your needs for support and peace, then by all means go, just remember the truth behind your drug use."

December 8, 2006

Lawrence reported for his orientation. This client was put on Proposition 36 for possession of a narcotic substance. Lawrence is forty-two years old single male, half Japanese (Father) and half European (Mother). At this time in his life he lives with his parents. His drug of choice at the time was cocaine. I asked him why and/or how he was busted for possession. He mentioned that he was upset that his plans for opening up a motorcycle shop were thwarted because the city took his truck away, which had been broken down in the front yard for a period of time, due to it being an eye sore in the neighborhood. He stated, "I got really pissed off and used drugs to deal with my anger. I got caught sitting in my car."

I asked the Lawrence to tell me about his life as a child, adolescent, and young adult and how he related to his parents. His initial description was about his father who he referred to as "old school Japanese." His father was a mathematician and, therefore, his life had to be exact and have answers. His father made him take piano lessons and let it be known that school was of the utmost importance. He mentioned that both parents would hover over him while he did his homework. He said he was taught to accomplish things.

The client's mother also focused on school and would constantly monitor his behavior. When the client was twelve years old he got involved in a few fights while in middle school. He stated that once his mother got wind of the fights she transferred him (Lawrence) to another school where he was one of the few minorities. He got involved in a fight at the new school and he said the parents nagged him until he told them what happened. The client proceeded to inform his parents who he had fought with and his parents did the unthinkable: they went to the school to tell the principle what had happened. That incident alone marked the client as a snitch, and he would be beaten by his classmates throughout the school year. From that point on, the client shut down and withdrew into himself. He was afraid to make friends for fear of getting into fights and his parents finding out.

The client stated he began to use various drugs at the age of nineteen because he was with friends who used. After several uses, the client became empowered because the narcotics allowed him to forget about his old self and become the person he always dreamed he wanted to be. He did things he normally wouldn't do while being under the influence, such as give an opinion, talk to girls, make more friends, and feel more confident. For the first time in his life he expressed himself and said things and experienced things that he would have been afraid to do if he hadn't tried drugs.

As I gathered his information I began to put the pieces together. I explained to him that his need for empowerment, self-expression, and identity were not being met. His father's demands of perfection, rules, and forcing him to do things because he thought it should be done his way were stifling to the client.

The client explained to me that he received his first motorcycle at the age of twelve. To date, the client can put together a motorcycle from scratch. He also mentioned that when he was taking piano lessons his mother would force him to practice a certain way. The client told me that at one point he somehow convinced his mother to play the notes several times for him. When the mother did, the client proceeded to play the exact notes his mother had previously played.

Hearing the client's last comment inspired me to pull out my Whole Brain Thinking® Model chart. I explained to the client that "the reason you clashed with your parents is that your parents have a blue/green (left brain) preference which is safe-keeping, analytical, cost effective, and establishes procedures. You have a yellow preference (right brain) which is where one takes risks, breaks rules, infers, and speculates." In other words, the parents and the client saw the world from two different viewpoints. It was at this point the client really understood his past behavior with his parents and how he tried to constantly fight for his need for choice, self-expression, and identity. The client was actually amazed that we had uncovered this bit of information. He stated he actually felt relaxed and had a sense of relief. He mentioned that he was grateful and is looking forward to gaining more information about himself.

*****

The next client today: David, a gay thirty-nine-year-old bi-racial man (black father-Mexican mother). David stated he started drinking when he was twenty-one years old. He was arrested for possession of cocaine and put on Proposition 36.

I asked David if he would like to learn about his drug problem. I mean, really understand it so he can be aware of it and, hopefully, do something about it. He said he would like that very much. I explained to him that the information I was about to share with him would change his life and empower him. He said he was interested.

He began to explain his home life by describing his father. He mentioned he hated both of his parents for how they treated him as a boy. He stated his father said cruel comments to and about him while he was growing up. He said his father was a backyard mechanic whose interest was in auto racing. He said his father had these expectations of how a son should be and that he was an aggressive man who hoped his son would follow in the same footsteps. David stated he was not interested in sports but art, books, and academics. His father would praise him in public but then shame him in private.

David's mother, a seamstress, was what he referred to as a "bitch." He stated she would constantly yell at him in public. In her life, everything had to be perfect. If things were not as they should be, then David would pay for her non-perfect world. David continued to say that this pressure was endured until he got his first car at sixteen and then he stayed away from home as long as he could, usually until bed time.

As David got older his father asked him if he was "one of them." David lied but when his father found out later he would have nothing to do with him.

David used drugs a lot during his early twenties. He discovered how they could numb feelings and put him in a place where he felt emotional safety for the first time. This is the Superman Syndrome. David also became a people pleaser. David would sacrifice himself for the sake of not ruffling any feathers for fear that people would not like him as his parents did. When I explained his behavior to him, David, for the first time, came to the realization about how his past relationships with his mother and father were the root cause of his drug problem and his lack of self-worth. I informed David that given time he could learn how to heal his past wounds and change his current behavior.

*****

Keith came back for his second session. His initial visit exposed that he was the only male child left in the family. He mentioned that his mother and two sisters spoiled him. Therefore, he believed he was entitled to anything as a boy growing up. As an adult, he continued to have those beliefs.

Unfortunately, when he didn't get his way he would have a tantrum and use drugs to get back at the person who didn't give him what he wanted.

Now that Keith had a few weeks to digest this information he stated he couldn't wait to get back to tell me how his life has changed. He proceeded to tell the people at the AA/NA meetings that his drug problems are over. He mentioned, in his way, that people need to look at themselves in order for them to have a chance to stop using drugs. Of course, the treatment counselors didn't want to hear about it. Nonetheless, Keith stated he could not sleep the night before our session because his life had changed so much that he couldn't wait to tell me the good news. He stated that he is not acting like the spoiled brat of the past. He is treating his child and his girlfriend differently. He stated that he wants to stay on Probation in order to stay in contact with me. I said that staying on Probation wouldn't be necessary for us to stay in contact. He walked away smiling and laughing as he went through the waiting room and out the double doors. I always glance at the people in the lobby to see their reaction toward a man leaving the Probation office with a smile on his face.

ACKNOWLEDGEMENTS

I dedicate my first book to my mother, Pauline Pinkston-Oden. I express my deepest appreciation to the person who has been there for me from the beginning and continues to be. She has been the cornerstone for her eleven children for the past sixty-six years.

Above and beyond raising her own children, she has also impacted the lives of hundreds of foster children that came through our home. It was her constant presence that allowed me the confidence to begin my journey and to take chances, knowing I would always be her son and loved whether I succeeded or not.

How I saw myself as a child and what I did with that self-image began at home. This image or perception of myself that was established at home allowed me to take chances, fail, and succeed with the utmost confidence. I was never told by my mother or my siblings that I couldn't or shouldn't take risks. Yet, somehow through pure naiveté or ignorance, I always managed to have the courage to take those chances without the worry of failure. Well, this book was not planned; this journey began some time ago because I saw the impact I had on my clients by sharing this information. Hence, the birth of this book.

I'd like to acknowledge and thank my siblings, who have been a constant support throughout my life. No one ever said "You can't." I thank you all both individually and collectively: Wentworth (Earl), Mila, Terry Ann, Chester Wayne Jr., aka Moose (now deceased), Eric Vonn, Markel Scott (my twin), Christopher Wade, David Bryon, Aaron Delaney, and Brett Hamilton. Also, my son, Michael Jr., who makes the challenge of parenting worthwhile.

I'd like to thank William Stierle, my mentor and friend whose lengthy discussions and valuable input over the years has allowed me to create ways to contribute to the lives of others; in ways that are both enlightening, meaningful, and effective.

I'd like to show my gratitude to George Abich, my spiritual advisor, for continued personal insight and guidance about my career, personal life, and future ventures.

I'd also like to thank Deborah Drake, my editor, for making this book make sense and allowing me to be more creative and effective as a writer.

A special thanks to our graphic designer, Erica Staton, whose creative talent and patience produced the vision of the book cover.

Lastly, I want to give a deep appreciation and special thanks to my business partner, friend, and ally Alina Ugas and her daughter, Shiovan, whose strong spiritual beliefs and authentic concern allowed me to convalesce during my lengthy treatment for lymphoma and for championing the notion that I publish this book during this juncture in my life—because no one ever knows what life has in store for them.

Every time I work with a new client or a group in a recovery setting, I am bringing all of you with me to support me and the individual you will most likely never meet. The presence I have in the world doing what I do the way I do it, is because of all who have touched my life, which is my own "Hero's Journey."

I take none of my life experience or those who help make me who I am for granted.

BIBLIOGRAPHY

Myss, C. (2002) Sacred Contracts: *An Awakening Your Divine Potential.* Three River Press, New York, New York

Herrmann, N. (1995) *The Creative Brain.* Quebecor Printing Book Group, Kingsport, TN. *The four-color, four-quadrant graphic and Whole Brain* are *registered trademarks of Herrmann Global, LLC.*

Bly, R. (1996) *The Sibling Society.* Addison-Wesley Publications, Reading, MA

Rosenberg PhD, M.B. (1999) *Nonviolent Communication*: A Language of Compassion, Puddledancer Press, Encinitas, CA.

Stierlie, W. (2005) Corporate Culture Development

http://www.caldrug.org/prop36.html

U.S. Census Bureau, Current Population Survey, Annual Social and Economic Supplement, America's Families and Living Arrangements: 2012, Table F2. Family Households, By Type, Age of Own Children, and Educational Attainment of Householder: 2012, Internet release date: November 2012. See http://www.census.gov/hhes/families/data/cps2012.html.

RESOURCES

The Final Step offers training programs for groups and organizations that can always be customized; such as behavioral modification, thinking style, team building and in the areas of:

Drug and Alcohol Education; Understanding Drug Dependency
Understanding the trauma of childhood socialization, the origins of Drug Dependency and the impact that it has on self, the family and society.

Anger Management
Anger does not have to negatively impact your relationships and career. With anger management classes, you can learn how to deal with your anger to improve the quality of your life and your relationships with others. We will assist you in identifying the source of your anger, unhealthy behaviors, and negative thoughts.

Continuing Education Unit (CEU) Providers by the Board of Behavioral Sciences

*   Drug and Alcohol Education; Understanding Drug Dependency
*   Spousal/Partner Abuse-using (NVC) The Needs Based Method®
*   Anger Management for Young adults dealing with resentment and abandonment issues

A Skill Building Group for young adults - Transitioning into your future!
Transitioning into your future is a program developed for young adults who want to learn how to survive independently and successfully. Group is 10 weeks, interactive meet-up focusing on building adult living skills such as: *Preparing for College*

Support Group for Family or Professional Caregivers of Older Adults with Dementia/Alzheimer's Disease

Support for the Caregiver during the care-giving process is essential to the Caregiver's mental and physical well being.

To learn more about Michael S. Oden and his work as a Speaker, Counselor, Consultant, workshop facilitator and his training programs, please visit

www.michaeloden.com
www.theneedsbasedmethod.com
info@michaeloden.com

FACTS ABOUT THE AUTHOR

Buzz about the author / What's being said about the author

Questions that was answered about the author

1. What can I be counted on for/what are my strengths in your experience of me.

You show up, when it matters and even when it doesn't. Your constant presences is reassuring and meets my needs for emotional safety.

2. What three best words best describe me in your experience of me?

Dependable (reliable), Non-judgmental (open minded), Understanding

3. What makes me memorable to you?

Your witty yet sarcastic sense of humor and your cool as a cucumber demeanor.

Shiovan Cote

I 'm happy to help with this project. Thank you for including me.

1. What can I be counted on for/what are my strengths in your experience of me.

I see you as being fiercely loyal. I knew almost immediately that you would be a lifelong long friend. I remember several years back when Mark and I were having problems, and you told me that you would ALWAYS be there for me because you knew I didn't have much family for support. It still brings tears to my eyes when I think about that conversation. You were so in tune to what I was going through, that I will always remember it as if were just yesterday.

2. What three best words best describe me in your experience of me?
You are a risk taker, insightful, compassionate . . . you can be stoic but at the same time, funny as hell! You have this amazing ability to be humorous even in what appears to be the darkest of times.

3. What makes me memorable to you?
What makes you memorable to me is probably your odd sense of humor and I mean that in only an absolutely positive way. Also, your interest in others and your very authentic interest in helping those around you who might be suffering.

Hope that helps. Let me know if I can do anything else.

Love you always,
Adela Mcvicker

Hello Michael . . . Here you go!

What can I be counted on for/what are my strengths in your experience of me?
You can be counted on for being compassionate, insightful, and funny. You have an amazing ability to see the best in people and the skills to help people overcome their limiting beliefs about themselves.

What are three words that best describe me in your experience of me?
Emphatic, Insightful, and Understanding.

What makes me memorable to you?
Your sense of humor and your ability to make people feel comfortable. You have an easy going style, when you're teaching a class or coaching a

client, you have the rare gift to help people see themselves in a new light. You offer them hope and compassion.

I LOVE YOU Michael Oden!!!!!
Suzanne Rock-Stierle

To: Michael Oden, answering these questions about you was the easiest part of the book journey!

1. What can I be counted on for/what are my strengths in your experience of me.

Always being there for me. Putting a smile on my face when I think the world is coming to an end. Knowing just what to say to ease an individual's mind

2. What three best words best describe me in your experience of me?

Understanding, non-judgmental, honest and a true friend (oops that's four)

3. What makes me memorable to you?

Your wonderful sense of humor, allowing me to be myself. Teaching me to grow to my full potential as a person, mother and friend.

Michael Oden you are my best friend and the best business partner a women will ever have. You have taught me so much. My daughters and I will be forever grateful to you.

All of my needs are being met with our everlasting friendship,

Alina Ugas

P.S. Lymphoma didn't stand a chance with Shiovan and I nursing you back to health.

July 05, 2013

To Whom it May Concern;

It is my distinct pleasure to write this letter of reference and recommendation for Mr. Michael S. Oden. He was an "A" student of mine in a master's degree program course at National University. He was a leader in the class, exemplifying high academic standards as well as personal and professional ethical conduct.

I have remained in contact with him over the years and in 2012 recommended him for a position as an advisory board member for criminal justice at National Polytechnic College in the City of Commerce. He was accepted and provided good leadership examples and recommendations.

I also invited him to be a guest speaker in one of criminal justice classes and his reception from the students was extremely favorable. The academic director suggested inviting him back for several more presentations.

He has also contributed a chapter in my forthcoming book, The ReEvolution of Gangs.

His dedication to the value of education and the professionalization of criminal justice practitioners exceeded the norm, going above and beyond with no expectation of personal gain. I am therefore very pleased to highly recommend Michael Oden for any position in which he would be contributing directly or indirectly to an agency's educational objectives.

I may be contacted at 310-490-7441 or by email at 4mrusss@gmail.com

Sincerely

Dale L. June (Signature Electronically Produced)

Dale L. June (MA) Adjunct Professor, National University
Former Special Agent, US Secret Service

02/10/2013

To whom it may concern:

Michael Oden has been under my supervision for the past 2 years as a supervising deputy for the Proposition 36 caseload and is currently supervising the 290 PC sex registrants. His responsibilities included writing reports and making evaluations that were relevant to the compliance of each client.

What I appreciate most about Michael is his commitment to his job, especially his clients. He is one of a rare breed of Probation Officers who I have witnessed over the years who actually takes the time to converse and encourage each and every client that he has been assigned. Over the past several years, the Probation Department has been moving toward the method of treatment as opposed to that of being punitive. I can honestly say, Michael has been practicing his methods with his clients long before the directive became mandated. There were times when I had to explain to Michael that he need not spend so much time with his clients due to the amount of clients he was supervising at that time and other administrative responsibilities that needed to be fulfilled. I decided it was in my best interest to give the clients what they so desperately needed and that was for someone to listen to them. Over the past several years, I have received letters from clients informing me about how much they appreciated what Michael has done for them.

As a Probation Officer, Michael has gone beyond the expected responsibilities by taking on cases that are not assigned to him. There were many instances when I asked Michael to investigate and write a report on a Probationer when the workload became overwhelming for a staff member. Michael is always ready to assist me and his co-workers

It is apparent to me that Michael enjoys coming to work so he can add to the lives of others and that he wants to better himself by obtaining a Masters Degree in Counseling. I believe it's a perfect match and I don't know why he didn't enroll sooner because it seems like natural fit. I can honestly say National University is getting an enthusiastic and promising student.

Sincerely,

Andrea Washington - Supervising Deputy Probation Officer

Michael S. Oden, M.A., Behavioral Specialist

July 21, 2013

Letter of Recommendation

To whom it may concern:

I, Dr. Sandra Baca, am the Director of "About Face" Domestic Violence Intervention Project. I have had the pleasure and opportunity to know and work with Mr. Michael Oden for the past 2 years, who is a Probation Officer for Los Angeles County for 290pc (sex registrants). Michael and I have a working relationship where our clients share psychotherapy and group sessions together.

As I have gotten to know Michael on a professional level, I discovered the passion he has for his occupation. Michael has this quality to enlighten and encourage those around him, including his clients. I was delighted when Michael decided to obtain a Masters Degree in Psychology in Counseling. This further supported my belief in how Michael wanted to improve his educational level, as well as, his ability to assist his client's.

While working with Michael, he has continued to display an excellent rapport with staff members, as well as, his clients. Michael has great verbal and written communication skills. Due to Michael's experience as a Probation Officer and Therapist, he has the opportunity to share his insight with others who can benefit.

I am confident that Michael's insight and passion will benefit your organization. Please to do not hesitate to contact me if you have any questions.

Respectfully Submitted,

/s/ Sandra G. Baca, PsyD

_____

Sandra G. Baca, PsyD

Michael S. Oden, M.A., Behavioral Specialist

July 23, 2013

Re: Michael Oden

To Whom It May Concern:

I am writing this letter to inform your organization that I/We, Dan and Bradley Yourist, have known Michael Oden for the better part of three years. Our organization hired Michael to conduct process groups/counseling sessions with a certain criminal population. Michael has demonstrated that he is willing to do what is asked of him due to his passion for his vocation as an educator/lecturer.

During the time that our organization needed a qualified individual to perform group sessions for high risk sex offenders on parole, Michael was the only individual who would take on this daunting task. Michael served these individuals for several months with surprising results and the feedback from these clients were nothing but positive.

Michael demonstrated that he was consistent and reliable when it came to reporting for his assignments. He was well organized, efficient, and extremely competent with the material he presented to our client's. Michael also had an excellent rapport with our clients who can be quite demanding due to their long criminal history. Due to Michael's empathy and diplomatic approach with these client's after the initial session, we did not have to concern ourselves with any impairment that may potentially come in his direction.

In sum, I highly recommend Michael for any position or endeavor that he may seek to pursue. He will be a valuable asset for any organization. If you have any questions, please do not hesitate to contact me

Very truly yours,

BRADLEY J. YOURIST

136

Printed in the United States
By Bookmasters